The Hardest,
not the
Worst Year

A Widow's Journey

KATHIE POWELL

The Hardest, Not the Worst Year
A Widow's Journey
Kathie Powell

Copyright © 2024 - Reflek Publishing

All Rights Reserved.

No part of this publication may be reproduced, distributed, or transmitted in any form or by any means, including photocopying, recording, or other electronic or mechanical methods, without the prior written permission of the publisher, except in the case of brief quotations embodied in critical reviews and certain other noncommercial uses permitted by copyright law.

Disclaimer: The author makes no guarantees concerning the level of success you may experience by following the advice and strategies contained in this book, and you accept the risk that results will differ for each individual. The purpose of this book is to educate, entertain, and inspire.

For more information: hello@kathiepowell.ca
ISBN Paperback: 978-1-962280-33-4
ISBN eBook: 978-1-962280-32-7
ISBN Audiobook: 978-1-962280-34-1

Here's a Gift before You Begin

To download your FREE Workbook Companion to *The Hardest, Not the Worst Year* please visit:
www.kathiepowell.ca/thehardestnottheworstyear

This book is dedicated to John Peter, the love of my life, my best friend, my lover, my biggest supporter, and my everything. You inspired me in life, and you continue to in death.

I also dedicate this book to my three daughters, Sarah, Rayna, and Jill; their husbands, Aaron, Jay, and Jarret; my grandchildren, Jack, Mason, Levi, Brody, Nora, Gus, and Zach; my sister, Maggie; and my dear friend Kim.

Each one of you in some way has helped write this book, some by your own words, others by listening to mine and encouraging this book. But mostly I dedicate this book to each of you for being here with me without judgement through the hardest year of my life.

Contents

Introduction 7
Chapter 1: How It All Began 15
Chapter 2: In Sickness and in Health 25
Chapter 3: Till Death Do Us Part 37
Chapter 4: The Last Goodbye 53
Chapter 5: Coping: Walking through Life's Changes 79
Chapter 6: Fear and Grief 93
Chapter 7: Going through His Things 101
Chapter 8: Jack's Moment 107
Chapter 9: He Asked for Little 121
Chapter 10: Signs 127
Chapter 11: The Promise 137
Chapter 12: My Journal 141
Chapter 13: Where Did She Go? 159
Chapter 14: Losing a Father 173
Epilogue: The Last First Time 189
Let's Connect 199
About the Author 201

Introduction

You may have picked up this book because you are grieving or know someone who is grieving. Or you may have picked it up by accident. There are no accidents. This book is a book about grief—my grief. It's not all sad, and it's not all happy. It's a real story about love and loss.

This is my journey about losing my partner and the aftermath of what life has become since he died. Something I thought after the death of my husband, John, was that I didn't sign up for this. It wasn't supposed to be this way. But . . . there is also a *but*. This particular thought nudged me to look at our wedding vows, and I soon found out that I did. We did. We both signed up for this and so much more.

If you are married, you signed up for some pretty hard shit, but also some pretty amazing shit too.

My Wedding Vows

I, Kathleen Berenice, choose you, John Peter, to be my partner, my love, and my friend. I choose you to walk beside me through all of life's joys and challenges. I promise to support you and stand by you, celebrating our successes and facing our struggles together. I vow to be there for you in times of sickness and in health, in times of plenty and in times of need. Where you go, I will go. Where you live, I will live. Your people shall be my people and your God my God. I promise to love you unconditionally, to cherish our bond, and to honour our commitment for as long as we both shall live.

To be honest, the day we said our wedding vows was not the best day of my life. I think my best day up to that point was when I met him. When I think of our wedding day, it wasn't really beautiful. He was beautiful. Me . . . I didn't get the dress I wanted. I didn't know most people at my wedding, and my dad offered to pay John at the altar when he gave me away, just in case John was having second thoughts. (Thanks, Dad.) But are any of these the reasons we got married? No. We got married because we were young, we were in love, and we just wanted to be together forever.

Regardless of what the day looked like, it felt right. It was right. It was the beginning of our beautiful, ugly, best, worst, and full-of-love days to come. It was the beginning of our forever. I didn't pay attention to the vows; I didn't feel them. We both repeated them, and we were married. Goal achieved. It wasn't until about twenty years after we were married that I began to understand the depth of meaning behind the words we spoke to each other. Real life, hardships, struggle, sickness, joy, and success—we lived it all. Each step on the journey was a life lesson in love and commitment. We lived and honoured our vows through to the very end.

Introduction

Our forever looks different than I envisioned when I first told him we were forever. Forever is our love. Love doesn't die because our earthly bodies die. Love is forever. We are forever.

The truth of the matter is that I have a sad story. This book is about grief. It's about my grief and my journey this last year, the hardest, not the worst year of my life. This book is a story that I never thought I would ever write, let alone live through. The sad truth was I had no road map to what life was going to be like after he died. I have no sense of direction and get lost all the time. He was my true north. This is a story of finding my way amid such darkness.

So, yes, there's going to be sadness within these chapters. This is a book about a real relationship and real loss. It's about pain, sorrow, surrender, and love. If you're a grieving person who might feel lost in this new reality, I want you to know there can be a big, beautiful life after loss. It's not easy; it's really hard. Within these pages, you will uncover humour within the sadness, pure joy, anger, hope, bad decisions, good decisions, and how I found my new purpose. You won't find stages to go through or a checklist. I can't tell you how to grieve or how to feel. What I can do is share my journey with my story of grief in the hope that you feel seen and it ignites a passion in you to live and love your life right where you are, with little regret.

A moment I want to share: About a year after John died, one morning after I had a sleepover with one of my grandsons, we went for breakfast. It was our thing. We went to a big chain restaurant and ordered. We were in the far corner when an older couple came in. They were seated at a table just across from us. They were beautiful. He was a veteran; he wore his military ball cap and zip-up coat with his regimental patches sewn on. He was using a walker and looked more fragile than she. She gently guided him. You could tell they were regulars because of the way the server interacted with them. They were laughing and talking to one another, and I could not help but stare. Tears came streaming down my cheeks. I quickly wiped them away because the server brought us our breakfast. I felt overwhelmed.

I asked her if I could buy this couple breakfast, and she said, "Of course. Do you want me to tell them that you bought their breakfast?"

I said, "No, but please . . . when we are gone, without identifying us, can you say thank you?"

She smiled and nodded.

My grandson asked why I was buying them breakfast. I told him that that old man was a veteran just like his dad and papa; he served our country. That I was grateful for what they both sacrificed. I know it's not just the soldier who serves; the loved ones left behind serve too. It's a different kind of sacrifice I know well. Also, I said that love was a beautiful thing, and I wanted to honour what they had because Papa and I would never get there—not in this reality, anyway. As I smiled, tears rolled down my face. I got a giant hug and a kiss on my cheek.

He said, "I like that, Grandma. I love you."

"I like that too, and I love you more . . . grandmas always love more."

The realisation that we will never grow old together—like really old—still stings.

This is not a "how to grieve" book. It's not a book to tell you what you should and shouldn't do. The book that I share will show you that grief is unique. Your grief is a mirror of your relationship with the person that you lost and loved. Big love equals big grief. How your grief shows up is your experience.

This is a book to show you that in the most devastating year of my life, I did some of the most courageous things I've ever done, mostly because I had no choice. But I still did them. It's about the things I had never done before yet succeeded and the things I did and failed at. This book is about the last twelve months of my life. It's not all sad; it's not all happy. It's real life. I hope you enjoy it.

"We were so young without
a clue of what forever
meant"

Chapter 1
How It All Began

Our Story

Now I know this is a book about grief and a story of loss, but there is room for joyful memories. Grief carries with it beginnings and endings. Grief is about love and loss. Grief carries with it more than pain; it carries memories that we can sit with. Memories that will make us smile and cry. Grieving is the natural response to the pain of our loss.

This is part of our story. Here is a snapshot of our beginning. Maybe in reading this you won't feel so alone.

This is a story of love at first sight . . . for me anyway. It was more than a physical attraction. It was something I had never felt before. It didn't scare me.

It was a hot day in June of 1979 when I met him. I remember exactly what he looked like and what he was wearing. He was wearing Levi jeans, a Patricia's T-shirt, and Adidas gazelles. His face was tanned and round with a short blond military haircut, pouty lips, and those intense hazel eyes staring back at me with a look of disdain. I was wearing my combats, without a jacket and a white V-necked tee, with rainbow suspenders (*Mork and Mindy*-inspired), and I had my mirrored aviators on the top of my head. I thought I looked so cool.

A friend of each of ours grabbed me and said, "I have the cutest little *Picklie* for you!" I was intrigued. (What is a Picklie, you ask? "Picklie" is a nickname for men in Princess Patricia's Canadian Light Infantry)

When our friend introduced us, John simply said, "I should throw you in jail for defacing the queen's uniform." Oh my gosh, I was in love.

Okay, so I was off to a great start. I just turned around and walked out, trying to look as cool as I hoped I looked. I had the intuition that I would win him over. For some reason, I just knew we were meant to be together, and right there and then, I set my sights on him.

I remember standing outside my barrack (a building that housed about twenty to forty bunk beds for the people who came to do summer courses), and he was running by. His legs were long, and so was his stride. He was a good runner. I could see from a distance the focus he had. He was beautiful. I swore that he was going to be my husband one day. I just knew it. He had no chance.

When we met the second time, I was not looking my best (unlike the first time—ha-ha!) It was in the afternoon, and we had just taken part in an exercise (exercise = the Militia (Today called Reserves) plays war games and does training with the Regular Force). The night before, I had decided not to sleep with my mosquito netting because I didn't want to wreck my hair. Bad decision! I woke up the next morning with my face swollen and covered in bites. I never felt a thing that night, but I sure did in the morning. At this point, my hair could not save my look. The captain I was driving for put this shiny gauze on my face to cool it off and soothe my very sore, swollen skin. It also highlighted the hideousness of my face, making it much more noticeable.

Guess whom I saw? John, of course. There he was, looking as sharp as always in his uniform, while I looked like a dishevelled mess. "*Hi, it's me, shiny, bumpy-faced me, the woman you will spend the rest of your life with.*" (Of course, I didn't say that out loud—I tended to talk inside my head a lot at the beginning of this relationship.)

John sort of smiled that smile he had that said, "Oh my God" as he looked at me in horror and then just spoke these words to me, "Hey, you look like you had fun!" and giggled a little as he walked away. I believe he felt it was just punishment for what I was wearing when I first met him. Cool.

Our next meeting was when we were fighting fires. Destiny and adventure awaited! I was my normal-faced self again, wearing my uniform, pressed and polished. (Let's just say I stopped being a rebel in uniform and began to wear it properly and proudly after our first meeting. John was a good influence.) For this next adventure, I was the driver taking a group of soldiers he was with to a field to fight brush fires around the camp. When we arrived, I left the truck and went with him (I was not letting this chance get away.) To this day, I don't know who brought the truck back to camp, but it wasn't me, and I didn't get in trouble for leaving it. The things I got away with back then. A charmed life?

As we were walking and talking, we diligently searched for any sparks on the ground that could create a fire. We still had an actual job to do besides getting to know each other. (Can I just say some sparks were flying between us, too.) We talked about lots of things. I really liked him. He was so smart, funny, and kind. I asked him questions about himself because I was genuinely interested in what my future husband was like. I heard all about his future plans and his career goals. He was so sure of himself and what he was going to accomplish. I listened intently as he told me his story, and then he looked at me and said, "Thanks for asking me all about myself. I don't usually talk this much, but I would like to know about you."

Gulp. Oh shoot. What should I say?

"Me? Um, I'm seventeen years old. I have no real plan except that I'm going to marry you." (Inside my head again.)

I felt shy and somehow out of sorts. He took my hand; he could see I was stumbling with what to say. (*Oh my gosh, he is perfect*, I thought.)

"Just tell me where you're from and why you are here doing this army stuff."

I laughed. "I'm from Moose Jaw. My dad was in the army, and that's the place he decided our family would live forever. It wasn't my choice to live there—I was twelve. I joined cadets because I wanted to do something to feel closer to my dad.

Chapter 1

It didn't work out that way, but I soon found the militia and joined. I really like it, and I get paid to do it! Also, it's a lot of fun. I'm here because I like the army—doing drills, firing weapons, and leading and training recruits. Also, I've met some of the most fun and amazing people. Are you fun?" (I already knew he was amazing.)

He laughed and said he could be fun, but he was here to further his career and train for his jump course in the fall. He didn't really have time for distractions; he needed to focus on training.

"Okay, cool, but what about us?" (Inside voice again.)

He invited me to a party he and his group were having that night. So no distractions, huh? Now was my chance to charm him so he, too, would realise we were meant for each other. I was going to be a big distraction but in the best way possible.

That night, my girlfriend and I got dressed and put on some terrible spray that smelled sickeningly sweet . . . oops. We put on outfits we thought were kinda cute (we didn't have much to choose from—we packed for army camp) to go to this party. When we arrived, John quickly got me a drink. He was so hospitable. I have no actual idea what it was, but it was strong and terrible, and I drank it. He said he had to leave for a bit and left me with a young guy in a suit, who I found out was a reporter on assignment for a paper and hated doing army stuff. I was with this guy for what seemed like an hour and was starting to get drunk. This drink was strong. Where the heck was John anyway? I excused myself from the reporter and went outside. There was John with a girl. What the actual fuck? They were getting a bit too cosy. Shit was about to get real for her. Who was I? I had never acted like this. But I was determined. I knew he was my forever, even if he didn't know it yet. He was soon going to learn.

I was never confrontational, but at that moment I was. He was making a mistake, and I needed to correct it. I walked over and proceeded to tell this young woman off and tell her he was mine. (Oh my, I was full of myself and "bottle courage.") I think I scared her because she left quickly. Then I thanked him for the drink and told him it was time we got to know each other better. I believe I kissed him first, and it was not good. I caught him off guard. So again, I seemed very confident in myself and proceeded to explain kissing. (I know, right?) Let's just say he knew how, but he went along with my education, and we kissed a lot, and he was very good. We were very good.

We didn't discuss why he and that other girl were together until a few conversations later. It didn't matter to me. Anyway, from that point on, we were a pair. I was his girl. He was my forever.

We spent the next several days taking risks to be together. We shouldn't have, because he could have gotten into way more trouble than me. Being young and in love can make even the most dedicated soldier falter and do foolish things. The CliffsNotes version is: we went skinny-dipping in the camp outdoor pool late at night (now that's a story); we also went

Chapter 1

AWOL one weekend (absent from the armed forces without permission) and spent two nights in Saskatoon getting to know each other better (I was now eighteen and had my birthday a few days prior—again, another great story). We never got caught, thank goodness. Charmed life—or someone watching over us?

After only ten beautiful days, he asked me if I was planning on going to Winnipeg in the fall. (That's where he was stationed.) I said yes, I was going. I was going to go wherever he was. Truth be told, I had no idea what I would do, but my sister lived there, and she would be a great resource for helping me get settled. (And as it turned out, she was.) Once he knew I was moving to Winnipeg, he looked at me, and he said softly, "I think I'm falling in love with you."

Wait, what? Thank you, Jesus, that he said it because I was too afraid to . . . my courage and forwardness had left me in the midst of this, and now I was feeling very vulnerable and insecure. I was in love with him, and I was too afraid to say it for fear he might reject me. I had never been in love like that before. I stumbled and smiled so big with tears running down my face, saying, "I love you too. I don't *think* I love you; I know I do!" (So romantic.)

Oh, and in case you were worried: John accomplished all his goals and more. He was focused on his goals, but he always put me first. From the beginning, we encouraged and supported each other's goals and dreams. We believed in each other.

The Hardest, Not the Worst Year

When I think of this memory, my heart smiles, and so does my face as tears stream down my cheeks. This is grief. This is love. These next chapters are the story's last leg of his journey. There will be joy, pain, shock, anger, hurt, confusion, learning, service, and love.

"*Our beginning*"

Chapter 2
In Sickness and in Health

We All Have a Terminal Illness, and It's Called Life

Ours is a love story full of passion, excitement, heartbreak, fear, anger, loneliness, togetherness, partnership, disappointment, and triumph. This recent chapter of our life brought me back to something we said to each other when we got married, something that didn't quite mean what it means today. There are so many chapters to our story, and this book captures my journey from losing John through my journey of grief over the last year. But first, let me take us back to before the bottom really fell out.

On November 29, 2021, my husband of forty-one years came in from the garage and sat down. I was watching the news (something I hardly ever do); it was about 6:00 p.m. He looked at me and said quietly, "I don't feel well." My heart sank almost instantly. He had never said that. Except once before, fifteen years previously, when he was having a heart attack.

"Like, not well, well? Should I call an ambulance?" I knew what the answer was.

"Yes," he said.

I walked over to him and kissed his forehead. "I love you," I said, as I dialled 911. He was in distress. I was so scared. I had to focus and make the call with my hands trembling and my heart pounding, trying to pretend everything was fine so he wouldn't worry about me.

He kept saying, "I'm sorry."

I kept saying, "It's okay. It's going to be okay."

I had never called 911 before. When he had his heart attack fifteen years earlier, I drove him to the hospital. I know, but we lived in the country on an acreage, and I didn't trust anyone to get to us in time. Plus the Edmonton Oilers had just won a big game during the playoffs, and the streets were chaotic . . . that's another story.

The 911 operator answered and calmly asked me what was wrong and where I lived. I stumbled through what I thought was happening, as my husband was trying to not pass out. I gave her all the information she asked for. She kept talking to keep me calm and checking in on him. He started to pass out, and the only thing I could think of to keep him conscious was for him to take long, deep breaths. I did the deep breathing I used in childbirth. It's all I could think of. We did deep, slow breathing together, and I asked him to keep looking at me, which he did. His eyes were wide, and his breath laboured as he did as I asked. The operator said I was doing a great job.

Chapter 2

She was so encouraging. I needed to hear her and not be alone. I was more frightened this time. Why was it taking so long for the ambulance?

We waited for what seemed like forever, and I couldn't understand why it was taking so long. We had a fire station just around the corner from us, but the ambulance was coming from the city. Two EMTs came into the house and took charge. I felt like everything was in slow motion. John was having trouble processing what was happening and hearing the EMT who was working with him. I interjected that he had trouble hearing. Once he knew, he spoke louder to John. John tried to answer the questions. The other EMT sent me up to get his medications. When I came down, I was starting to show signs of stress and maybe a bit of emotion.

The EMT to whom I gave the medication said, "You need to calm down. He doesn't need to see you upset." I was shocked because I wasn't crying, and I wasn't saying anything . . . but I guess my body language said otherwise. I felt like a child. Like he was going to say, "Don't cry or I'll give you something to cry for."

I took a deep breath and acted strong. All the while thinking, "Fuck you. My husband is having a heart attack. I know this to be true because I have been here before, and *I'm fucking scared, okay!*" I told myself to take a deep breath and not to cry.

They took him outside—actually, I had to help him because he was staggering and leaning to the side, and I was afraid he would fall. The gurney was just past the front steps. They helped him onto it, strapped him in, covered him with a blanket, and put him in the ambulance. The one EMT who had been working with John told me to wait at home for about sixty minutes to let them get him to the hospital and then try to get in to see him. It was very iffy because of the pandemic whether I would be let in. My mind again was swirling. Why was this happening? He had been fine all day.

I turned and walked into the house. I was numb. What should I do? Who do I call? I didn't want to burden anyone. I didn't want to show I was afraid. But I called my daughters, except my youngest. She was only a few weeks away from delivering a baby, and I didn't want to stress her out. So I called Rayna and Sarah and they quickly drove over.

While I was waiting, I noticed the lights still flashing outside. They were still here. I thought they had left. I ran outside. No one was in the front of the ambulance; they were both in the back. I started to panic. I stood there waiting. Screaming in my head and too afraid to knock on the door. I waited.

Then one EMT came out, and I asked, "What's wrong? Why are you still here? What's happening?" He smiled and said everything was fine; they were just getting him ready to go. Like it was no big deal and I should relax. To them, it was no big deal. To me, it was terrifying. I thought something else had gone wrong. My mind went to the worst-case scenario.

Chapter 2

Then they drove away, and I sat on the ground and tried to comprehend what was happening. Nothing, no tears, no screaming, just numbness.

I went inside and waited while my daughters came to see me and help however they could.

One of them offered to drive me to the hospital, and at first, I thought, "No," but then realised I could use someone. I was in no condition to drive.

The rest of that evening is a blur. I was so glad they let me in. I can remember being with him trying to be brave. The whole time I was inside, Rayna waited in her car. I can't imagine how scared she was. I texted her updates. I watched as things started to escalate, and they made the decision that he had to be moved to the Royal Alex cardiac intensive care unit.

They told me not to go there for a few hours; again, they had to get him settled, and they were not sure I would be able to see him.

Rayna and I went home, and I don't know what we did. Then we drove to Alex; again, it was a blur.

When I arrived, Rayna stayed in the vehicle to wait for me. She was so loving and kind. By some stroke of luck, they let me in to see him. He was in the critical care unit with a nurse right outside his private glass room. I had to cover up fully and sanitise my hands after each step of dressing in the required items. I couldn't go near him.

He asked so sweetly, "You can't come any closer? Not even a kiss?" So I sneaked over and gave him a little kiss on the forehead, then quickly went to my spot at a distance. I could only stay a few minutes. It broke my heart to leave him, but I knew he was in the best hands. I prayed in my mind. I begged God to save him, just like I had so many other times before.

I don't know if I trusted God to grant me the answer to my prayer this time. Had I been good enough? Faithful enough? Had he answered my prayers too many times? I closed my eyes and tried to trust.

It was almost three o'clock in the morning when we got home. My daughter stayed with me. She was such a blessing. I am forever grateful. We didn't sleep much, if at all.

I ended up getting a terrible cold. I felt it coming on when we were driving home (maybe stress); I felt so sick the next day and for a few days after. I couldn't go up to see him. I had to stay home. We got to FaceTime, which helped. He had surgery to put stents in and stayed in the hospital for four more days.

When he got the okay to come home, my son-in-law came with me to pick him up. Again, I was so grateful for the help. I don't think I have ever been so happy to see John. My prayers had been answered.

When we got home, John asked me if he could have a bath (he never had baths). I thought it was odd, and I checked with him twice, but it was what he wanted. So I ran him a hot bath and helped him in, and I washed his hair. It was a bit of a challenge helping him out because he was exhausted. I put him to bed.

Chapter 2

Afterward, I went downstairs, sat, and started to feel. I felt relieved, I felt scared, I felt angry, I felt helpless, I felt alone, I felt betrayed. I felt overwhelmed.

I was tired, but the truth is that he was the one who always did all the heavy lifting around the house. Now it was my turn. This experience showed me how much I didn't do. Now my routine had changed drastically. My day consisted of taking care of him and everything else. I organised his meds and made sure he took them at the right times. I walked the dog, I shovelled the snow, I shopped for groceries, I cooked the food, I did the dishes, I took out the garbage, I got the mail (when I remembered), and I took care of him. None of it felt like a burden.

The night after he came home, I sat in the quiet and started to feel again. I felt ashamed, I felt grateful, I felt sad, I felt humbled, I felt love, I felt scared, I felt lonely, and I felt useful. I now really understood what he did for us and all the things I had taken for granted.

I took care of him, for a change. This was hard on him. I cannot speak for how he felt, but his eyes showed me, and a few times, his lip would tremble as he told me how much he appreciated everything I was doing. I could see the pain, the disappointment and frustration. Dear Lord, I don't think I ever told him I appreciated what he did from day to day. He just did it all. It broke my heart again to see him struggle to feel like himself again. I think both our hearts were broken.

The Hardest, Not the Worst Year

One year later, our life was very different from what it had been before his heart attack. His healing process had been challenging and hard for him to adjust to. It was hard for both of us. It wasn't happening the way we expected. We were both frustrated and could get short with each other now and then. But our compassion and empathy for each other always showed up. Then we talked it out and listened to each other, and we kept walking faithfully together.

One day, for the first time in a year, he came out and helped me shovel. It was amazing. I didn't care how much he did; he was out there doing it. It felt good to work together. This may seem like it was a small step, but it was such a big one. I knew it still frustrated him, but he did it. We did it together.

I didn't know what the next day had in store, but I knew that I loved him. I was grateful he was there; he still had that sarcastic sense of humour and could make me laugh like no one else. He was my biggest cheerleader, and I was his. We truly *got* each other. We were enough as we were, to have and to hold, for better or worse, for richer, for poorer, in sickness and in health, and to love and cherish each other always.

After almost forty-three years, those traditional vows we had spoken to each other when we were just kids now held so much meaning and so much truth. When we said them on our wedding day, we didn't understand the profound meaning those words would hold for us. Tears stream down my cheeks as I write this, feeling so much gratitude for the man I married and the children we had together. We are all here for each other. I love this family so much.

Then, less than a month later, things would take another turn, and more words from our wedding vows became a reality—and not at all in the romantic way you envision: *"Till death us do part."* This is when the bottom really fell out.

What I know now: John had cancer. He never quite got his footing after his heart attack. He never quite caught his breath. He suffered for over a year but never complained. He went to the doctor to find out what was wrong, but they were looking at his heart until December 28th, 2022, when it was very clear it was not his heart. Our perfectly imperfect world suddenly changed. The free-falling without a parachute had just begun.

"Our last few months together"

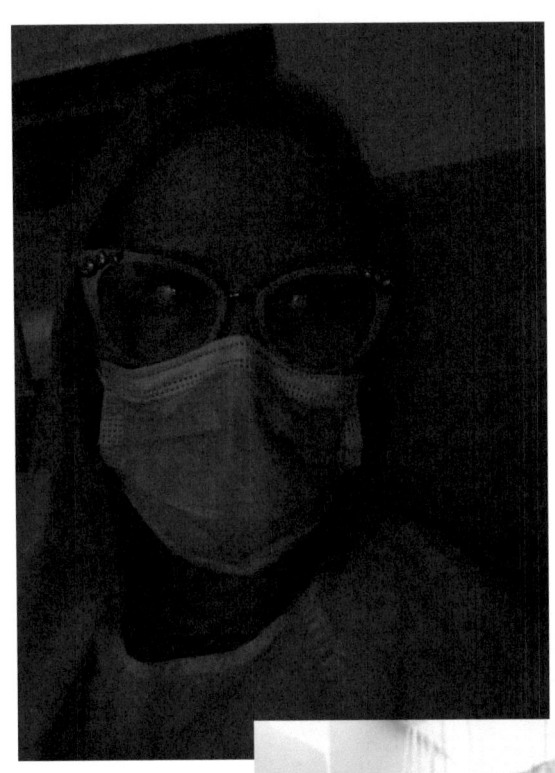

Chapter 3
Till Death Do Us Part

The Things They Don't Tell You

No one told us these would be the last twenty eight days of John's life.

The things they didn't tell us were the clear facts. They couldn't tell us how long or how bad it really was, besides advanced stage 4 stomach cancer, but they did guess he wouldn't make it a year. In situations like this, they don't tell you a lot because you can start to lose hope.

John's illness was advancing very quickly. They didn't tell us how hard it was going to be on everyone watching someone we love die. They didn't explain that he would find it hard to look into my eyes and see me see him dying. They didn't share how we as human beings know how to die.

They didn't tell us how scary and exhausting it would be to be in charge of all his care at home. They didn't tell us how devastating it would be to watch him die. They didn't tell us this would be the longest and shortest twenty-eight days of each of our lives.

They don't tell you how to move forward when it's all over and your broken heart has to try to pick up the pieces of your broken life. They don't tell you because they can't. Death can be inevitable, but it is not always predictable, and timelines aren't always accurate.

We knew John didn't have long to live, but we didn't know how short the time would be. This all started on December 28 at our GP visit to see why he was just not feeling right. We didn't know that this was the beginning of the end of his life.

We were informed early on that he had ascites, which was usually associated with cirrhosis of the liver, heart failure, kidney failure or infection, or cancer. In the beginning they danced around the idea that it was cancer because everything else looked fine. No one told me that John would tell me he knew he was dying. No one told me that I knew at that moment he was dying too. No one told me how a person can manage to keep breathing when their whole world is shattered.

On December 31, they removed six litres of fluid from his abdomen. He sat up and said he felt so much better. It wasn't till January 8 that the doctor informed us of his actual diagnosis: he had palliatin metastatic gastric carcinoma—they told us in simple terms "stomach cancer." It was in the upper stomach and had spread to the peritoneum (the serous

Chapter 3

membrane that lines the abdominal cavity). Later we would find out it had spread to his lower intestine. They also told us he wouldn't see an oncologist for six to eight weeks. I asked why. They said everything was so backed up.

I spoke with his internist, who very frankly said to me, "Kathie, there is nothing the Cross can do for him. He is too far gone." I remember thanking him for being so honest but feeling sick to my stomach. John only lived sixteen more days after his official diagnosis.

John's only wishes were that I be there holding his hand when he died and that if it was possible, he wanted to come home to die. He got those two wishes granted. I remember him being so weak and tired, but he had to be able to walk up at least fourteen stairs and walk at least around the ward. He looked at me and laughed and said, "Funny. I have to get strong enough to go home to die." He did it, even when he had nothing in the tank. He powered through to get home. He was determined.

Now we, his family, were the caregivers. We were more than a little nervous. We were going to oversee everything: his care, his comfort, his nursing, and his meds. We were told it would be fine, that they had it all sorted, and the meds we were going to give him were by mouth, no injections. We had bubble packs made up to keep it simple for us. Home care would be there, and eventually palliative homecare would take over. They told us we were set; they didn't tell us we were in over our heads.

Waiting for the ambulance to take him home was hard on John. He was tired, and the waiting was taking its toll on all of us. He also had to do an oxygen test to prove he needed the oxygen, which he had been on since his third day in the hospital. No one could explain to me why this had to happen, why a doctor couldn't just vouch for him. The test was very hard on him. After waiting from 11:00 a.m., we did not get the news that the ambulance was on its way until 6:00 p.m. We were sort of excited and mostly scared. This was Thursday, January 19. The hospital team hooked up with the oxygen people, and they were going to meet us at home to set him up. They set up home care . . . but told us as we were leaving that home care wouldn't be there till Monday, and this was Thursday. We were going into the weekend. No one told me if you are dying, you need to make sure it's not over a holiday weekend or any weekend. I was in shock; they were sending us home without help. How could that be? I didn't want to alarm John, so I said nothing, but my girls and I were very distressed about the whole thing.

They told us it would be fine. They didn't tell us the reality of what we were stepping into. They said, "It will be hard, but you will have so much help!" But we weren't going to get help just yet, because it was close to the weekend. WTF!

On the ride home in the ambulance, John looked out the window to take it all in. He knew he would never see the city like this again; this would be his last time. My heart broke a little more watching him. No one told me how much my heart would continue to break. I sat beside him, terrified of what I was about to take on. Could I do this? Was I prepared? The answer was yes, I could (we could) do this, but, no, we were not prepared. The hospital prepared us the best they could. Honestly, no one could have prepared us for what was to come. What we needed was a support system with someone who had been here before. We didn't know that an end-of-life doula existed, or I would have hired one to be there with us. But you don't know what you don't know, and they don't tell you when you don't know to ask.

None of my fears mattered when I saw the look on John's face when he saw the house. Whatever was to come from here on in, it was all worth it. It was something I will never forget. It was so beautiful; he just took it all in, and he looked peaceful and content. He was very quiet as he looked at our home.

He got to come home. At that moment, I knew we had done the right thing for him.

When we got there, the house was full of people: the girls, my sister, Steven our nephew, the firemen who helped bring him in, the EMTs, and Wendel our faithful dog. The oxygen tech person and me. Once John was settled into his new bed in the amazing room set up by one of my sons-in-laws Jay, Stephen, and Maggie my sister, he would again have to do a test to prove he needed oxygen. These tests were very taxing on his body. Oh my gosh, if I had known how hard it was for him, I would have objected, fought to have them not make him do it again. I'd pay for the oxygen. He had been through so much already. But I just watched, unable to say or do anything.

After everything quieted down, we let Wendel in to see John, and it was a sweet exchange. Wendel sniffed and nuzzled him, and John petted him like he always did. Wendel would spend a lot of time just outside the room on the floor because he was too big for the space on the carpet by John's bed.

John lay down and looked at me and sweetly said, "Thank you for doing this." All I could say was, "Anything for you . . . I would do anything for you," choking back tears. No one told me how I would love him even more through all of this.

There was a moment of something that was almost normal for him. John wanted to walk to the island and visit with Maggie and Stephen. He stood at first and then sat. He smiled and chatted a bit, and even had a Popsicle. I could tell he was tired, so I looked at him and he nodded (we didn't need to say anything), and we walked back to his bed. He lay down to rest and took it all in.

My sister sent me upstairs to have a shower and change. I heard some noise downstairs, and I ran down. John was throwing up. Oh God, no. They said if he started to throw up, it could mean a blockage, and that was not good. John calmly assured me it was probably the ride here and maybe the pain meds they gave him to help with the transportation. He hadn't needed any pain meds, and it might have upset his stomach. So I was like, "Okay, that sounds right." He was settled again. At around 9:30 p.m., I gave him his evening meds. He slept.

Chapter 3

I went up to have my shower, knowing my sister was there to cover for me.

All was quiet; I was sitting in his room, and then at around 11:30 p.m., he threw up again. I remember one of the firefighters who helped bring John in telling me to never hesitate to contact home care or them for help. So I called the twenty-four-hour home care line. John was so new to the system that she didn't have any information, so I gave her his health care number, and she pulled up his file. She listened as I spoke, cried, and asked for help. She called an ambulance and told me that because this was an "end of life" call, the paramedics would come without lights or sirens and would come in to give the care he needed and leave him at home. I was thankful because I promised John he wouldn't have to go back to the hospital again. The EMTs came and took good care of him. They stayed for an hour to make sure the antinausea meds worked. We settled for the night. He slept. Maggie was my backup, and I watched.

The next morning at 7:00 a.m. John's phone rang (wrong person to call—it took a while for that to get sorted out). Our homecare worker would be coming that day to see him and assess him. Thank you, God!

Then I got a phone call from our palliative care doctor's office, telling us our doctor would be there to see him next Friday. Wait, what? I asked why and told her about the ambulance and the nausea. She just said that was the schedule. Luckily, our case worker sent notes to our doctor, and the doctor showed up at 1:30 p.m. that same day. Our little miracles. All John's meds were changed, and he went from oral meds to injectables.

So our journey continued. Each day, we had to call for help, and they always came to help us. They changed his meds three times in the short time he was home. I didn't sleep as I watched him sleep and talk in his sleep; it was like he was working. He was so restless; I think sleeping was exhausting for him.

We wrote down everything we did, the time, and what we did. We documented how he was acting and feeling, and what he ate or drank, which was very little. He was quickly getting more distant and less able to talk. He slept more, and when awake, he would look at us and say what he could. He always told me he loved me and that I was doing a good job. Oh God, I prayed we did a good job. We told him from the beginning we would defer to him about everything, that he was the lead in this. We honoured that as best we could. He needed to know the time and what the schedule was if he was seeing anyone. He needed a sense of some sort of control. He needed to know what was happening. He was in a vulnerable position, and I did all I could to keep him updated on what was happening. I did all I could to keep his dignity because death is messy and unkind.

No one told us how to navigate his wishes, even if we didn't understand or agree with them. No one explained how we would tell his grandchildren they couldn't see him because he didn't want to hurt them or scare them. That it was too hard for Papa to see them because he loved them so much. No one told us how to sit with them in their pain because they didn't understand why they couldn't see him. No one could explain the depth of his love for them. These are things we navigated through, stumbled through, cried through, and are still getting through together, letting each of those beautiful children know how very much he loved them.

On Monday, he looked different. His eyes were different, and he was different. In the afternoon, we played music and sang to him while he lay with eyes closed, and I sat beside him singing. We loved to listen to music together (concerts were our thing), and he loved when I sang. He told me that day if the only thing he had left was being with me and I sang to him, that was all he needed. So I sang over him, and my sister and daughters sang harmonies in the background. I remember thinking how incredibly beautiful it was. No one told me about how beautiful moments can be even in the darkest of times.

Monday night was the worst. I had to increase his oxygen because he needed more; he was having a harder time breathing. We also had to change to a mask because his nose was so dry and scabbed from the oxygen. (They don't tell you about cream to use to help prevent that.) That night, he was very restless, pulling off the mask because it was uncomfortable, so I switched it back to the one inserted into the nostrils. I didn't care at that point; I just wanted him to be comfortable. No one told me that I would sacrifice his physical well-being (the pain from the scabs on his nostrils) for his mental well-being (so he could relax). He was talking much more in his sleep. He would wake, and it would take him a minute to figure out what was happening. I think one of his biggest fears was losing his insight into what was happening. It was one of mine too. The meds and dying take so much from you. I can only imagine how hard that must have been for him.

Tuesday morning around 3:00 a.m. he woke up, and we talked a little. I remember him drinking his Gatorade and thinking that it was a good sign; dying people stop eating and drinking. He was drinking! He hadn't eaten anything the previous day, and that day was no different. Most days, it took him a whole day to finish a bottle of Gatorade.

His home care coordinator came to see him around 9:30 a.m. because I had concerns about his legs and the swelling. She assured us he was okay and that there was no concern. She told us to start giving him his pain meds because it would help with his breathing. She also showed us how to move him in his bed because his legs were so long and he would get scrunched at the bottom of the bed. Why hadn't they shown us before?

At 1:30 p.m., his doctor arrived to talk to him about options. Because we had given him pain meds, he really had to concentrate hard. He spoke very slowly so that the doctor clearly understood what he wanted. Then the doctor gave him some options for compassionate comfort care. He gave him the choice of what to do to be comfortable and sleep but still be able to talk with his loved ones, or go into a deep sleep. John's choice was to go into a deep sleep until he died. John was done. The doctor sent the prescribed medication to put him into a deep sleep to the pharmacy. We had to wait for it to be filled. My son-in-law picked it up for us so we could get it quicker. No one told us how much medication we would have to return to the pharmacy for them to dispose of.

That afternoon, he moaned a lot and seemed agitated. I sang over him and held his hand; he seemed to settle a bit, at least for a while. Later, I noticed he was clammy but so cold and seemed very distressed. His eyes were partway open and cloudy-looking. I checked his hair, and it was wet; his back was wet. I started to panic. No one told us this was how it would happen. I got Rayna to call home care and his doctor. Rayna was told it was normal and not to overreact. They didn't tell us this was it. Strangely enough, I read something out loud to each of us that afternoon about what happens when someone is dying. It said some things about the dying person, and I also read that it would be harder on the caregivers. None of that came into our minds when we were going through everything. No one said how painful and scary this would be.

We had to try to make him comfortable (for us not him, we needed to feel we were helping him), so Rayna heated up a blanket to try to warm him. I took his temperature, and it was 35 degrees Celsius. It was going down. I think on some level, I knew he was in the end stages of his life, but my heart didn't want to believe it. I wasn't ready; none of us were ready. I begged the home care nurse to come, and she said she would be on her way by 7:30 p.m. Rayna's husband, Jay, had arrived with his new meds while I was still on the phone with the nurse. She told us to give the newest meds because they were anti-anxiety as well as sedating. This would put him into a deep sleep. He would relax. Terrified, Rayna and my sister gave him the injection (we always administered his meds with two people). Rayna told him exactly what she was giving him before she administered the meds. She gave him the medication at 7:12 p.m., and within minutes, he settled.

By the time the home care nurse arrived, John was actively dying. I was begging for help, telling him I was so sorry and that it wasn't supposed to be this way. I cried because I had promised him a good death. I felt like I was failing him; I was helpless in all this. He was helpless in all this. Then he stopped breathing. I asked Rayna, "Did he stop breathing?" Then he took a larger breath, and he stopped breathing for good. That was his last breath.

John died at 7:42 p.m. It was neither beautiful nor quiet. It was distressing, traumatic, and devastating.

They tell you it's harder for the people caring for the dying person, but they can't tell you what to expect. Like the birthing experience, things can be similar, but no two people will die the same way. No one told us how the quiet would be deafening. No one told us how much it would hurt. No one told us about the relief we would feel that it was all over for him.

To be fair, both our nurse and our doctor said they didn't expect him to die that soon. They weren't ready; we weren't ready. I knew he was dead, I knew him, I knew how he took his breaths and how shallow they were. I knew he wasn't breathing. Our nurse took more time to believe he was dead. When it was all over, she cried because it was her first home care death. We comforted her and hugged her. None of us were ready.

Do I regret bringing him home? No, because it was what he wanted. We cared for him the best we could and got help whenever we needed it as quickly as we could. We loved him through it all. We honoured him.

I sometimes sit and question: Did I do everything I could, did I honour him, did I keep him comfortable and safe, did I keep his dignity, did I do enough? All I know is that we as a family did our best, and that is all we could do. I pray he felt the love and care we gave him was enough. I pray if I didn't get it right that he forgave me.

We knew that on some level, this would be the hardest thing we had ever done. Each one of us, especially John, we just didn't know how it would really feel. No amount of preparing, reading, or education will ever take the pain away. The truth is when someone you have loved for a lifetime dies, there is pain.

There are things they didn't tell us because they couldn't tell us everything. Death and dying are not the same for each person. I am grateful for the care and compassion my husband received by our broken, overworked health care system. They deserve our support and our help to make things right for them and for the next families facing health crises.

John Peter, thank you for bringing out the best in me and for trusting me with loving and caring for you till the very end. I will always love you.

Now I want to talk a little bit about a "good death." Isn't it what we all want? I cried because I thought I failed John somehow. I didn't know what dying looked like, even though he tried to prepare me.

Here is the truth: some die with no pain in their sleep, some doing something they love, and some die with their person holding their hand. Many people don't get their dying wishes granted because they have never communicated them to anyone. Death, dying, and grief are subjects we don't like to talk about. It's uncomfortable, and it's scary.

Well, if I go by what John asked for, he had a good death. He had the death he wanted. He was at home, his dog by the bed, loved ones caring for him, and I was holding his hand. He got everything he asked for. A good death reflects what the dying person wishes. Death is not romantic or pretty. It's messy, devastating, and real. By asking questions and honouring the dying person's wishes, we can take some sting out of the whole event. We as the loved ones watching, sitting vigil, will have pain and experience the trauma of the loss, but in that, we can know we gave them what they wanted to the best of our ability.

So please start the conversation with your loved ones. Don't leave it till it's too late.

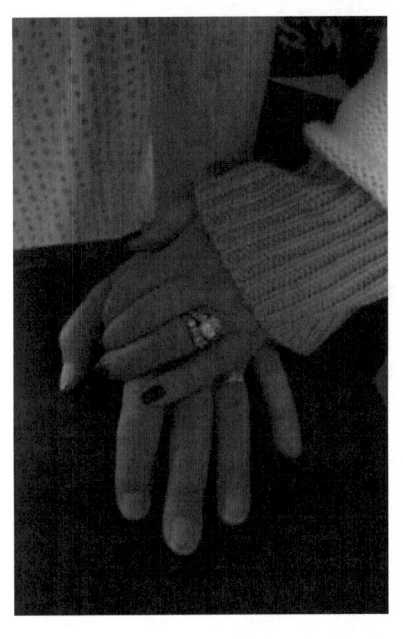

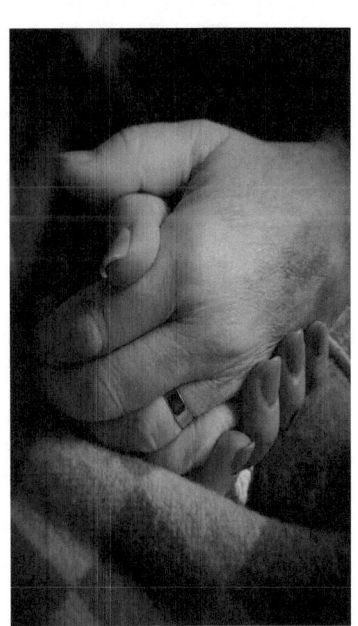

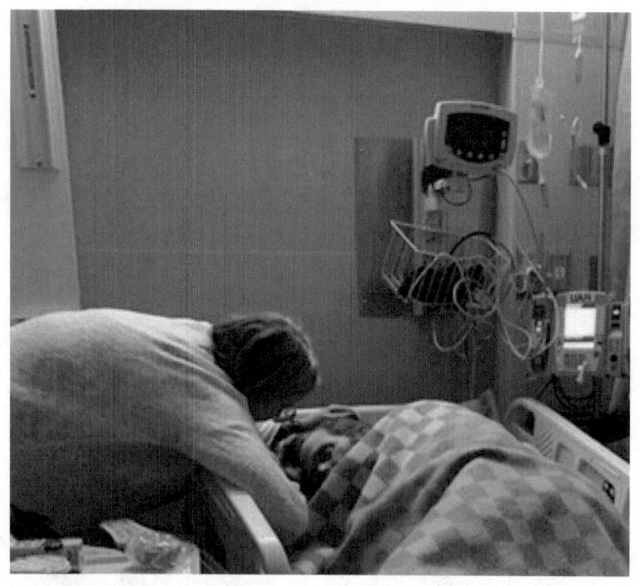

"Those last moments"

Chapter 4
The Last Goodbye

In Times of Struggle

This part is a blur for me.
I remember thinking that when John died, we weren't going to celebrate. How the fuck do you celebrate something like this?

Planning the funeral of the love of your life is one of the most beautiful but cruel things some of us will do after a loved one dies. Many of us have to sort out a funeral or celebration of life only days after losing our loved ones. This is a time when we are generally numb or still in shock. It's not the best time to make decisions. The truth is, John didn't want anything. We talked a little about his funeral but not much. I remember telling him we would keep it small to honour his wishes. It would be simple, just like he would want. We needed something to help us say goodbye. He looked at me weakly and said, "Whatever you need to do, babe. I won't be there." God, I hated when he said that, even though it was the truth.

Earlier (I'm not sure of the timeline; like I said, most of this is a blur), I called the crematorium people to let them know John had died. They were so kind and so gentle. They said that they would be there within an hour, but if we needed more time, they would give us what we needed. I told them an hour was enough time. But was it? I didn't know. I didn't know what to do with myself, let alone him or anyone else. Did we just sit with his body? His spirit was gone. Here is where some people wash their loved ones' bodies and dress them in the clothes they had asked to wear. For some, family and friends gather around, hold hands and sing, or recite meaningful memories of the person who died. We sat all around him, silent and weeping. I cut a lock of his beautiful hair, removed his ring, and kissed him goodbye. I now know some things we could have done. But you don't know what you don't know.

The man who came to get John called me before they arrived letting me know he would be there within the hour. I asked if he was okay with dogs, and somehow Wendel's name came up. He said he loved dogs and asked why we named him Wendel . . . it turned out the man who came to collect John and bring him to the crematorium knew Wendel Clark—that's who Wendel was named after, John's favourite hockey player. Well, this man had met Wendel Clark and told me about doing a training camp with him back in the day. He said he was a really good guy.

As I listened, I smiled and said, "This seems right, that someone who loved hockey and met Wendel Clark is coming to get John for the final leg of his journey."

I don't know if I called our pastor first. I don't even know what I said, but he asked me if he could come and be with us just for a few moments. I said, "You don't have to. That's okay."

He said softly, "I will be there shortly."

I'm so glad he came. He arrived very quickly. We were all so numb. I don't really remember the conversation. I just remember the hug. Our pastor is a tall man whose hugs are legendary. In that one moment, I felt safe. I told him we weren't going to do anything; we wouldn't have a funeral because John didn't want it. Our pastor listened and softly and wisely said, "This is not for John. It's for those whom he has left behind." Oh man, that hit. But how did we say goodbye? How did we do this?

We did it with lots of help and teamwork. Our pastor sat with us. Got a team of volunteers ready. Gave us contacts for printing up the cards to hand out and set up a simple coffee bar with John's favourite cookies. We wanted something simple to honour John. Pastor Jono gave us direction on how to make it flow but gave us the freedom to create what we felt would honour John. He told me that he thought I should speak.

Below are the words I spoke with my beautiful son-in-law, Aaron, by my side, holding me up. To honour his father (not by blood, but that is how they felt about each other, they were father and son), he carried John's maroon beret up with him as he stood beside me. Honestly, the two of us held each other up. It's something I will cherish till my last breath. John would have been so proud.

Here are the words I spoke that afternoon not to John but to those who came to say their last goodbyes. I had already said everything I needed to him:

> I'm here like many of you to honour John. The love of my life. Yes, there is love at first sight. I experienced it . . . in the depth of my being, I knew he was my forever, and in time he knew I was his forever.
>
> I remember the first moment I saw him, the sound of his voice, what he was wearing, his smile, and his light. Poor guy had no chance against me . . . I was determined, and I'm so glad he didn't run away from us; he ran *to* us. He was bold enough to say he was falling in love with me after a short ten days. I'm so glad he did because I wasn't going to tell him I loved him for fear of rejection. Gosh, I loved he was a no-fog, straight-talking kind of guy. Nine months later, we got married, had three babies very quickly, and created a real life together. It wasn't perfect—there were some really hard years—but we never lost sight of our love, even in the midst of some challenging years. There were also so many good, amazing years. The good always outweighed the hard. We moved through our marriage with hard work, dedication, respect, love, laughter, friendship, and faith—a whole lotta faith.
>
> I'd like to share this message I found in my notes while looking for something else. It's from John; he

wrote it in 2018. I think it describes who we came to be after our almost forty-four years together.

"We might look at things a little differently, but we share the same vision. Cut the crap, love each other, drama is not welcome, always count your blessings, and bless as many as you can. Life can change at any moment. Faith will see you through that change. Yours forever, John. God bless."

I know he would want to thank each one of you for being here and each person for what they brought to his life. So . . . thank you. He would also want to thank the people who surrounded us in our time of need. He was overwhelmed by the outpouring of love and kind words. He received so many messages from people, telling him what he meant to them and thanking him for the impact he had on their lives. He responded to as many as he could. Please know he read them all, and his heart was full of the love you showered on him. I am not going to name names or all the details. The list is too long, and I would be devastated if I missed someone or something . . . grief gives you brain fog. If I haven't thanked you in person, I will get to you. Also, thank you to everyone who came from out of town, sacrificing time and money to get here. Thank you for all the love and support. I honestly don't know how we would have gotten here today without you.

But I know he would ask that I share this: thank you to the broken health care system full of caring, hardworking, dedicated doctors, nurses, nurses' aides, home care, EMTs, and palliative care individuals who helped keep him safe and comfortable on this the last leg of this his journey here on earth.

John wasn't about this sort of thing, a large gathering in his honour. Example: His birthdays were always set up for the grandkids—what would they enjoy.

He didn't want to be the centre of anything, really. He was more about cheering others on. He was my biggest supporter. He was always there, proudly watching in the wings. But today, you are the centre, my love. I realised after speaking with our amazing pastor and friend Jono that this was not for you, John. This is for us, those who love you. So here we are . . . celebrating you, J. P. You are the centre, babe. So what do I say about a man I loved so deeply that when he died, he took a huge part of my heart that died with him, but I have also kept a huge part of his heart with me. The pain I feel is deeper and more gut wrenching than words can express. It takes me out at the knees, takes my breath away, and it hurts into the deepest part of my being. Anguish is what I feel.

But . . . let's get to what John expected for today.

John felt very strongly about seeing the one and giving a person in need a leg up without needing or wanting recognition. It was never done for acknowledgement; it was for the person who needed support. He always felt it was important to respect their

Chapter 4

privacy and love them without expectation. He always said, "When you give a gift with expectation, it isn't a gift; it's a business transaction." He taught me so much about love and about giving back.

The last few weeks of his life, we talked about our favourite memories and our love. We got the time to say all the things we felt needed to be said and heard. He said this time was our miracle. He never asked for the miracle of healing; he only asked for a little more time with me and his family. We also talked about today and what he wanted . . . what he wanted was for the people who thought about him to turn their thoughts to these two organisations that support, help, and empower women and their children. These organisations are Adeara Recovery Centre and Kaleo Collective.

Adeara offers hope, healing, and restoration from addiction, crime, and trauma. It is unique because children are allowed to stay with their mothers during their healing. It's not just about healing the woman; it's also about healing the family. This program has been around since 1998 and requires our donations to keep it running.

Kaleo is an organisation that is about supporting single moms. Again, it's not just about the woman; it is about her children. Kaleo empowers women to be self-sufficient and successful. The goal is to create sustainable families, to break the cycles of poverty, and provide practical tools and strategies.

This organisation requires our donations to keep their programs running.

Both of these programs help build strong communities. They help break the cycle of poverty, both financial and emotional, through amazing programming. As well, these organisations give their children a fighting chance to break free from generational traumas. If you have the means, please donate whatever you can; no gift is too small. There is information on both of these amazing organisations at the info bar.

I want to share these verses because this is the kind of love John believed in and practised daily, and it flows well with his message.

First Corinthians 13:4–7: "Love is patient and kind. Love is not jealous or boastful or proud or rude. It does not demand its own way. It is not irritable, and it keeps no record of being wronged. It does not rejoice about injustice but rejoices whenever the truth wins out. Love never gives up, never loses faith, is always hopeful, and endures through every circumstance."

But without the next verse, which was actually written first (the above verse isn't complete), this verse goes before and is very significant.

First Corinthians 13:3: "If I gave everything I have to the poor and even sacrificed my body, I could boast about it; but if I didn't love others, I would have gained nothing."

Chapter 4

We are made to love one another because he first loved us, cry with one another, laugh with one another, celebrate, and mourn with each other. We are here to encourage, support, and lift each other up.

John's favourite verse . . . he had it put on his last Harley. Funny story: I had a new wedding band made for him by my friend Sonya, a beautiful rose gold (to match mine), and I had his favourite scripture verse put in it. But I was wrong . . . I could have looked at his bike to get the information, but no, I just went with my gut. John 3:15 . . . kinda the same but not: *"That everyone who believes may have eternal life in him."* John believed.

John 14:6: Jesus answered, "I am the way and the truth and the life. No one comes to the Father except through me." John met with Jesus and knew him well.

John was at peace and knew where he was going. He said to me, "I have all I need, a little more time here with my family. Jesus gave me that miracle."

I will end with this quote from Brené Brown:

"Pain will subside only when we acknowledge it and care for it. Addressing it with love and compassion would take only a minuscule percentage of the energy it takes to fight it, but approaching pain head-on is terrifying. Most of us were not taught how to recognize pain, name it, and be with it. Our families and culture believed that the vulnerability that it takes to acknowledge pain was weakness, so we were taught anger, rage, and denial instead. But what we know now is that when we deny our emotion, it owns us. When we own our emotion, we can rebuild and find our way through the pain."

I will forever love you, John. Thank you for being mine and letting me be yours forever.

Sarah's (Our Firstborn's) Words

Good afternoon, everyone, and thank you so much for coming to celebrate my amazing father.

I still can't believe we're here. It's been eighteen days since he passed away.

I've spent the last eighteen days trying to figure out what to say today. What would be the best way to honour my dad? I've written so many different versions. I have no idea how to do this, but here we go.

As I'm sure you can understand, I've been dreading today. It makes everything more real, more final, if that makes any sense at all.

Our family has been walking through our hardest season since December 28. I keep playing these last weeks over and over again through my head.

The heartbreak we all felt. The frustration, the fear, the anger. But also, the love. I felt so much love, it hurt.

Holding his hand, tears streaming down our faces. It was a gift to be able to spend the time with him that we did, and I don't take that for granted for one second.

Chapter 4

I just want to remember every moment, every word he said—how his hair looked amazing the entire time. He had the best hair.

He told us he was at peace; he knew where he was going, and he felt free in that.

He sent this text to Rayna, Jill, and I on January 6, and I wanted to share it, as it was so special for us to receive this message from him:

"To all of you

I will always love you

Take care of you

Love your husbands and your children as they are gifts you deserve

If you can't love God, please love everyone as best you can

I'm at peace, any stress is not mine

Do not take ownership of anything that's not yours to worry about

We have a bit of a journey to finish

I want to enjoy the ride." 🐎🐎🐎🐎

When we were at home with him, he wanted music; he wanted to hear my mom sing.

He wanted her to be right beside him. And she never left his side. They were so beautiful together.

If you're here today or watching online, you don't need me to tell you what a great man he was. You already know—he was such a great man. He loved my mom, my sisters, our husbands, and his grandchildren so well.

I wrote this the morning after my dad passed away and wanted to share it today:

"You died last night and I thought I was ready. I thought because we'd been told it was coming, because I'd told you how much I loved you, because you told me how much you loved me . . . that I would be ready.

"I headed home yesterday afternoon to have dinner with my husband and our kids, to help with homework, to spend a bit of time with them before packing a bag and coming back to you. But before I could come back, the phone rang.

"You were gone.

"I wasn't ready.

"These last weeks were nothing that anyone could have been prepared for—heartbreaking and so tragic. You knew from the beginning. You took every opportunity to let us know that you were at peace, your quiet strength apparent to everyone who came to care for you. Never complaining, making jokes, giving us the middle finger here and there, right up until you just couldn't anymore.

"Yesterday, while you laid and rested, we played music and sang to you. We took turns sitting with you and holding your hand, stroking your beautiful hair, breathing in every moment.

Chapter 4

"Last night, after you passed, we played music again and we cried. We told stories, and we laughed. We got angry, and we cried. We hugged. We cried. We prayed. You're no longer suffering. You're up in heaven, smiling your beautiful smile, knowing that you lived a life that touched and inspired so many. That you loved your family so well. That you will live on through the love, kindness, and service of your wife, your children (daughters and sons-in-law alike) and your grandchildren.

"Our hearts are broken. We weren't ready."

We loved him so much, and we always will.

Rayna's (Our Middle Daughter's) Words
Hi, everyone. I'm Rayna, John's middle daughter. Please bear with me as I try to make it through this.

I want to thank everyone for coming to celebrate my father's life. It's so beautiful to be able to look out and see all the lives he touched (and I know there are so many more than represented here).

I will admit, I was feeling this immense pressure— like I had to come up here and try to make you all understand who he was and what he meant to me. To us.

I felt this sense of panic, like how? How can I do that? I have to make them understand. They need to understand.

The truth is, I can't, and I don't.

So I won't . . .

Having a relationship with someone for just shy of forty years is something that cannot be explained or articulated in a three-to-five-minute speech.

Knowing, loving, looking up to, appreciating someone, going through life with someone for that long . . . I could write a novel, and it would only scratch the surface.

All I can do is thank you all for coming. For celebrating him and the part he played in your life.

In each one of you, who had any sort of relationship with my father, you carry within you a spark of his spirit, of who he was. I am allowing myself to believe that as we are all gathered here today, all those sparks . . . no matter how big or how small . . . are coming together . . .

His time, his love, his energy, his wisdom, his kindness, his service, his personality, his laugh, his compassion, and his wit are here with us now.

So instead of me trying to fumble through this speech . . . trying to put words to a love that I have had all my life . . . I want us instead to imagine those sparks we carry, coming together in this place. I can only ask you to try to visualise them maybe weaving together by threads, into a web that connects each one of us together because of him and who he was. His energy. What he left within each one of us.

Chapter 4

The law of energy, surprisingly, has helped me immensely in these early days of my own grief . . .

The law states that energy cannot be created or destroyed, it can only be transformed. Everything on this planet is made of energy . . . on the most primitive level, you have an energy source . . . everything around us. Every cell. Every atom. That is just a fact. To think that when we die, our energy cannot be destroyed, only transformed . . . it brings me great comfort.

Thinking of the people and connections and relationships here and how my father's energy is still here. With us. My dad's love, his generosity, his heart of service, his laughter, the way he took care of us . . . that energy will always be here.

When I visualise these sparks, I can see them glow . . . it is so bright. It makes me think that *that* is his legacy. It lets me catch a glimpse of the magnitude of his impact. Of his energetic mark on this world.

I know without a shadow of a doubt that each of us was made better from having our lives touched by him in some way.

We all carry him with us, and that is so special. I want to ask one thing: protect that spark. That energy. Do not keep it to yourself.

Share it. Talk about him. Pass it on. Share stories and memories. Use the counsel and wisdom he shared with you, and apply them to your life.

My father would say, *"See the one"* —someone who needs help—and then help them.

That's how we honour him. It's that simple. See people. Don't look past them. Help without agenda, without seeking recognition. Just help because it's the right thing to do. Because that is love. And that is what my dad was.

When you experience a love so great, the loss will leave you completely devastated. The heartbreak and pain cannot be described . . . but I would experience it all over again without question because you cannot have love without loss

You get used to having that love . . . it's not gone, only in another form. Although I'd give anything to change how this turned out . . . at least I know it will never be gone, only available in a different way.

Jill's (Our Youngest Daughter's) Words

Dad, whenever one of my friends or coworkers met you , they immediately said, "Jill's your daughter for SURE." Our hair swooped the same way. We had the same weird, dark sense of humour.

I wasn't ready for you to die. How could I ever prepare for that? I wasn't there when it happened and when mom called me, I wasn't ready for the anguish bubbling up inside of me that only came out after I was off the phone.

Chapter 4

I can't believe I can't text you a hockey stick emoji whenever the Leafs (The Toronto Maple Leafs—John's favourite hockey team) score a goal anymore (or send a poop emoji when they lose). Or ask your opinion on a news story. Or hear stories about your time in the military. Or hug you. Or just know you're there. You were the best dad. You were the best papa.

Jill read a poem by John Updike, "Perfection Wasted".

Here is the first line and if you would like to read the poem in its entirety, you can find it by googling it. It is beautiful.

"And another regrettable thing about death is the ceasing of your own brand of magic, which took a whole life to develop and market"

Dad, there is a you-shaped hole in my heart now.

Each one spoke from their broken hearts. They shared their father with each person there. They shared their pain but, most importantly, their love. I can't remember the moments we spoke. What I can remember is looking up at the faces of the people who came to pay their last respects to a man who meant something to them, a man they loved. It was a beautiful sight. I know he would have thought it was too much fuss, but it wasn't. It was all about love, honour, and service, three things he prioritised in his life. He was worth celebrating.

The funny thing was, I was so afraid that no one would come. A weird fear, but I didn't want the room to be empty. He was such a good man.

The room was full. People came from all over: soldiers who served with him, men who knew him in a way I would never know. They came to honour a man whom they served with and whom they loved. I got to hear stories I had never heard, but the resounding themes were of honour, service, love, and generosity.

It was a beautiful service; I now see why it's called a celebration of life. We played all his favourite music. The playlist was really good, and Sarah did a beautiful slideshow. It lined up perfectly with "Against the Wind," by Bob Seger, one of John's favourite songs. The worship band that played had people in it whom John had mentored and who loved him. It truly was a celebration of life. His life was worth celebrating.

A friend sang and played "Photographs and Memories," by Jim Croce. The song John requested we play on Monday afternoon—another message he gave us, one we didn't figure out until a bit later, that soon he would be only photographs and memories.

Take pictures, my friends, and videos, and record each other . . . you will want to hear their voices again and again. When we walked out, we requested they play the intro to "Smoke on the Water," by Deep Purple. It was something I knew he would smile about. We truly celebrate the man he was and his legacy.

Chapter 4

What I know now: Sadness and grief are distinct emotions, each carrying its weight and complexity. While sadness may be a transient feeling activated by various life events, grief runs deeper—it's a profound longing for what has been lost. Amid grief, we often find ourselves wrestling with the pain of separation and the uncertainty of what lies ahead. Yet within this darkness, there is also the potential for growth and self-discovery. Through the process of grieving, we confront our vulnerabilities and confront the harsh realities of life. This journey isn't always smooth or linear; it's marked by moments of despair and confusion. However, in the middle of the pain, there is also an opportunity for healing—not in the sense of erasing our grief, but in learning to live with it. As we navigate through the depths of grief, we may stumble upon hidden resilience and courage within ourselves. We may discover new sides to our identity, new ways of coping, and new sources of strength. It's a journey of acceptance and adaptation, where growth often emerges from the darkest corners of our hearts. So, while grief will never leave us, it becomes a companion on our journey—a reminder of the love we carry and the resilience we've gained.

I need to share about the urn. Let's step back a bit to the days when John was in the hospital. One morning, Aaron was driving me, and we were talking. I was probably crying and trying to sort through things like his urn and what we would do next. I wanted it to be built by hands that loved him, hands that had been influenced by his love.

Aaron said, "Jay . . . Jay is an amazing woodworker. You should ask him." Then Aaron said with great wisdom and love, "Kath, he is still alive. Be with him right here, right now. I know you need to plan. We've got you. Go be with him right now; you need this too." He was right, so right, but my brain was kind of out of control. I was so worried about the future that I wasn't living in the present, and I needed to get back into our life what we had left.

Here is the story of the urn in Jay's own words:
It was mid-January when you asked me to make an urn for you and John. Of course, I said yes without hesitation, but I felt anything but confident. A deep sense of self-doubt kept me from developing a plan until, much sooner than any of us expected, I had no choice. The design for the urn came out of me all at once. I sketched it out in around an hour on January 25.

By January 27, I was able to find the wood I needed, a wide board of veneer-grade black walnut for the case, Spanish cedar for the linings and tray, and black limba for the lid panel. I used cocobolo rosewood from my personal stock for the banding, thumb catch, and feet.

I began work on January 28, having decided to use only hand tools for the entire process. The boards were resawn by hand, the thickness and dimensions determined using hand planes, and all joinery was cut without the use of power tools. Every surface was prepared with edge tools. No sandpaper was used at any point.

Hand tools have been a focus in my woodworking for years. Because they're so much quieter, music has a constant presence in my shop, and since my process involves many repetitive movements, it has always felt meditative for me. Time spent woodworking becomes time to think while one part of my brain is intensely focused. Every moment in my space was cathartic. Every act and every choice is therapeutic.

Before making this urn, I had only cut six dovetail joints. For the lid and back corners, I chose a simple design, while on the front face, there are seven dovetails on each side. In groups of three, two and two, they represent your seven grandchildren. This turned out to be an ambitious choice, both for my skill set and the amount of time I had to make it.

Over the next ten days, every possible moment was spent in my shop. I made steady progress until the morning of February 9, when Rayna helped me with the glue-up. I was working with a type of hot hide glue that cures fairly quickly, but even so, it was late afternoon before I was able to start planing the outside surfaces and cleaning up the joinery.

Because I needed to deliver the urn by the following afternoon, I chose natural finishes to avoid any strong odour of solvents or varnishes. That night, I was in my shop until 2:00 a.m. applying walnut oil. The next morning, I applied a natural paste wax scented with copal, frankincense, and myrrh, buffing and burnishing it to a satin lustre.

The urn was "finished" at 12:00 p.m. on February 10. I took a few photos before getting ready to bring it to you that afternoon.

This project that I gave to Jay, I knew it would be done with so much love and attention to detail. That man worked relentlessly to get it just right. He achieved his goal. The urn is smooth and gentle; feeling it is soothing to the touch. To me, the grain of wood reminds me of what you see when you look at the beauty formed from erosion on rocks over time. It's a portrait of loss and the wearing away of the human body but not its spirit. The building of this piece of art, our urn (one day I will share it with him) took countless hours, pain, imagination, and courage. I see it in each piece that holds it together. It's simply the most beautiful, most perfect piece to hold his ashes.

Inside there is a little ledge to put things on. It holds a lock of his hair, which his grandchildren take out occasionally. His wallet and a Valentine's card he gave to me and my sixtieth birthday card, both in his handwriting. A Valentine's card from me to him; a letter to his mother in sympathy for the loss of her husband, John's father; artwork by his grandchildren; and a bracelet one made for him that read, "Papa." A letter from the PPCLI. A beautiful eulogy written by a dear friend who served with him in the military. His old phone; a Harley sticker; a Bob Seger CD, *Beautiful Loser*; his glasses and dog tags; his coins: VP, Airborne, Paradepo and a memorial airborne coin, a small airborne pin; his name tag; an open pack of hauls; and two LEGO guys. Our first wedding bands and his last band. Each holds a little piece of him. On top of it, I have the comfort cross Jay also hand-made for me, a little "Be bold," mug and a paperweight John gave me years ago that reads, "You are my sun, my moon, and all my stars," by e. e. cummings.

John would love that this is such a meaningful piece that doesn't shout for attention. It's not about that; it never was. It was about the legacy of love, and this urn represents him better than I could have ever imagined.

"Remembrance, a celebration of his life"

Chapter 5
Coping: Walking through Life's Changes

One Constant in Life Is Change

The weird things that take over your brain when you experience this kind of loss . . .

The night John died, after we spent time together as a family, I drove Sarah home. I went into the house, and her children, our grandchildren, were there waiting for us. It's a blur, really, but I do remember the hugs, the tears, and the love that surrounded each one of us. Those babies had just lost their papa; only Jack had seen him during his last twenty-eight days. As a family, they each had seen him on Christmas day, a day when he was visibly struggling. Levi saw him the last day he was home before we officially started the journey into the medical system for someone who was dying. I wish I could remember what I said to them that night, but I can't. I only remember loving each one of them and crying.

When I got back into my car, I started to drive, and then I started to scream. I didn't cry—I screamed. I screamed and pounded the steering wheel. I wasn't angry . . . or was I? I was depleted, devastated, and lost. What was going to happen now? How was I going to make it? Actually, how did I get here? How did I survive watching him die? Watching him leave me more as each day passed? For the last month, I had been dissociated from my pain. Now I had no distractions.

When I got home, my beautiful, kind sister was waiting. I think we just went to bed. She was as devastated as I was. She was there with me each step of the way.

When I got into bed, I tried to sleep, but all I could see were him and his last moments. I tossed, turned, and wept. How could someone live with their heart breaking? The pain was so intense at times, I felt it hard to breathe. I didn't dream. I wanted to see him in my dreams, but there was radio silence except for the sound of my muffled sobs. My nights were no longer peaceful.

In the morning, I got up and made my bed like a robot. I washed my face, brushed my teeth, and walked down the stairs. I walked by the room that held the bed and all the things we used to help him during his last few days here on earth.

I instantly said in a panic, "This all has to go. I can't have it here."

My sister and my son-in-law (son) Aaron were there and told me to go upstairs and that they would take care of it. I went up quietly. I sat on the bed, our bed. I looked around our room. It wasn't our room anymore; it was just mine. I fell into a heap onto the floor and wanted to scream, but no noise came out. Again, breathing was challenging, I was most likely having a panic attack.

"Please come back, please come back! I can't do this. I'm not okay. I need you."

I got up and walked downstairs after everything was done. The room that held the man I have loved for almost forty-four years was empty. There was only a rug. It felt cold and lonely. I felt numb at this point. I thanked my sister and Aaron for taking care of this for me. We all just had a moment. Then it was quiet. How could I carry on? I sat in the living room, looking into the dining room. Fuck, how was I going to work through this? How could I live without him? How could I ever go back into that room? How could I sleep in our bed? How was I supposed to do this? I didn't have a clue.

John knew me better than I knew myself. Days before he died, he looked at me and said, "Kath, get rid of the things you don't want. It's not going to matter to me. I won't be here."

"What? No. Why would I even think of that?" He just smiled and squeezed my hand.

"Oh God, he isn't going to be here." That thought didn't penetrate my heart until it had no choice when he died. It was just me now.

Well, shit just got real. I had to change the bedroom. Something drastic. I couldn't sleep in there. I could hardly breathe in that room. I struggled for weeks. I lay on my side of the bed with his side untouched. I still do. (Making the bed each morning is really easy now.) I couldn't lie on his side of the bed. I tried to help myself by putting the last things he wore under my pillow. I would hold them tightly as I tried to sleep at night. Begging God to let me sleep. I put a picture of him beside the bed, but then I had to take it away because it unsettled me too much. What was wrong with me? Girl, you just lost your husband.

After a few weeks of thought, I went to a lovely store in my area of town to see one of the designers. I told her I wanted to change my room. I needed to change my room. We booked a consultation. She was aware of John's death. She was kind and cautious, and always checked in to see how I was, to make sure I never got overwhelmed.

She came over, and we went straight to my room. I told her, "I want to make it feminine. A woman's room."

Her eyes lit up. "Wallpaper," she said. We went from there. Boy, did we ever. She took what I said and made it come to life in a way I couldn't.

Now this wallpaper is probably the most beautiful paper I have ever seen. It came in quickly, and the man who was doing the work did a fabulous job. It was gorgeous. It was full of large peonies with so much detail that I could even see a few insects here and there. I now had a glorious flower garden on my wall.

I sat on the bed and looked at it. It made me smile. I loved it. I cried when I thought of him. Would he have liked it? I think he would have, but I don't think we ever would have done it if he were still alive. The truth in all this change that I

Chapter 5

was creating is I had all the control. I didn't have to run it by anyone. It was my room, my choice, my decision.

I wanted a new fabric bed frame completely different from the dark wooden one we had. We found a simple style I liked in a very pale pink, almost blush-coloured velvet, to tie in with the beautiful curtains I already had and the wallpaper. I would need a new dresser and end tables.

Before anything was ordered, I took the bed apart and slept with the mattress on the floor. I took the bedside tables and the bed frame to the garage. I had to get it all out. I'm not sure why, but I really needed to have it all out. Maybe it was so I could get a feel for the room stripped down. Soon everything arrived, and the room was set. You might say it was complete, but it was not. It would always be missing something very important: him.

This change was difficult, even though I made the decision to make the change, and I don't regret it. I needed it. It is said that whenever we make a change, we lose something in the process. That's the way it goes. There is a form of grief in change. For me, I was afraid of losing something I had already lost. Afraid I was erasing him. I know that isn't true; you can't erase love. I will never forget or erase him.

The room looks different, but the memories are still here. Each night I invite him into my dreams. I have yet to meet him there. The door to my dreams is always open.

But before the bedroom, the first change I needed to make was to get a bigger couch, Wendel could hardly fit on the one we had with me on it. We needed to snuggle. A new couch it was. Yeah, John was right. He was right a lot.

I didn't like the couch we had, and so started the big change. My way of distracting myself from all this pain was to renovate my house. Then things started to unravel. Maybe fall into place . . . depends on where you are standing.

One day while I was sitting in a chair in the living room, I looked at the kitchen and thought, "Man, I hate the backsplash." That's when the renovation started. It took over nine months to complete. I did way more than the backsplash. I looked at the fireplace, and that needed a little refresh. Then the cupboards, which led to the countertops and taking out the old desk that was just useless . . . then came the floors. At this point, I had a huge anxiety attack. What the fuck was I doing? We were in July. How did we get here? I just wanted a new couch, a small change. Oh yeah. I'm a go-big-or-go-home person. So I went big.

At the time all this was going on, I had moments of complete breakdowns; it was a steady stream of incompleteness. Wait, what? What was happening was that I created on the outside of my life what I was so loudly shouting on the inside of myself. I was incomplete. (A friend pointed it out to me one day.) Each day reflected my incompleteness without him. Now I don't know if the spirits that be were at work in all this, but my renovation should not have taken till the first anniversary of John's death to complete—but they did. So you might ask: When it was finished did I feel complete? Nope. But we will get there.

Chapter 5

We all have ways of coping with our pain. Now most things aren't bad in moderation, but when they become an obsession or you can't stop . . . you might have a problem. Renovating my home didn't take away my pain, but it did distract me here and there for a moment. I would sit in the rubble and cry out to him, "Why? Why did you have to leave me? Didn't we promise to walk beside each other through all life's joys and challenges? This wasn't the way it was supposed to be. You knew how I coped; you understood me better than anyone. You gave me enough rope to climb up out of the pit for a while."

Occasionally, I would get a nudge or a moment when I felt him saying, "Babe, come sit with me. Feel it; stop numbing it." Then I would sit and feel the ache of losing him. I would look around and know he would love what we did here. Me on earth and him in my heart. This house is still our house; he is everywhere, in every nook and cranny.

Weirdly, the last bit of change happened so fast with really no issues. I would even say smoothly. Now it's done. Now I still sit with the pain of losing him and the joy of loving him. The reality of it. Changing our home didn't take away my grief; it just distracted me, but it also helped me with my healing. I made it. I get that it might seem like an unhealthy way to cope, but he knew me, and he gave me the green light but also the check-engine light to say, "Now we sit. Now we really feel, and now we really grieve." I undid my home because I felt undone, and now my home is a tranquil, peaceful place where I can feel my grief and my joy.

The truth is that I did numb myself on occasion, but grief won't be ignored. Amid all the paint and deconstruction, I had time to feel grief. I don't regret the changes I made; in fact, I love them. This home that he died in felt like a tomb, and I couldn't feel peace. I was itchy under my skin. I felt scared and unsettled. Now I have let the light in, and I know he would approve. The truth is just as he said: it didn't matter to him because he wasn't going to be here. What he really was saying in that moment was, "Trust yourself. Create what you need to continue in this life without me. And I love you."

Now renovation was not my only way to cope. I coped by numbing myself with food, an old favourite. At first, I didn't eat, but then it became my go-to. This is funny for someone who doesn't like to cook or grocery shop. I lived on frozen dinners and quick snacks like chips and candy. I even tried a meal delivery program that delivered meals you picked and could cook fresh each week. It only lasted a month, and it was hard because the smallest you could order for was two, and I was one. I did have leftovers, but it became too much for me.

Most days I would find myself outside the pantry with a handful of something stuffed into my mouth, not even tasting or realising what I was doing or eating. This happened when I felt overwhelmed with feelings and didn't want to face the grief. It has always been a way to cope for me. It's a battle, mostly because I have a very unhealthy relationship with food. (That's a whole other story.) Please remember: food has no morality. It's not good or bad unless that is the lie you've been taught. My other coping skill was keeping so busy I didn't have to think about losing him. I was too busy doing or learning other things. All these things only worked till they didn't. It would happen in the quiet moments, like when I went to bed at night. Everything would flood me, and I couldn't sleep. When I did sleep, I would have nightmares, and if I couldn't sleep, I would turn on the TV and go downstairs and get something to snack on . . . numbing myself with a screen and food.

I quickly learned this was no way to live. I need to work through my pain, write about it, speak about it, share it. When we grieve, we can feel ashamed because people have long believed that feeling grief and expressing it is wrong. We need to hide it . . . hence the unhealthy coping skills to hide and stuff down our feelings. Grief is nothing to be ashamed of—grief happens because you loved. Shame lives in the dark; it thrives there. Once I sat with, walked with, and carried my grief, I began to heal.

Healing doesn't mean you don't grieve. Healing means you feel your life; you learn it's okay to express joy and grief. You learn it's okay to feel and that grief is a part of who you are. Now I still have my moments when I numb myself with food and some shopping, but mostly I catch myself (it might be afterward) and I ask these questions: Am I hungry, bored, sad, or grieving? What am I feeling right now? If I'm shopping, I ask myself: Do I need this? Do I have something like this at home? Will I wear it more than once? I will take a five-minute break, go outside if it's not too cold, grab a journal and write out the answers, and listen to guided imagery. If I still feel the urge, then I may go for it. Heck, this girl likes to shop!

What I know now . . . with the no-demo-reno complete, my home brings peace to my soul. It doesn't feel as incomplete—or maybe I'm used to this incompleteness now. My next steps are to continue to navigate what this life looks like on the outside as well as on the inside in this unfamiliar place: life without him.

We cope to get through some hard shit, and some of the things we do can be more harmful in the long run. We can't get ahead of our grief; it's right there, deep within us. It's not buried, it's not hidden, it's wearing a mask until it isn't. Till it pours out messily, making everyone uncomfortable. Grief is not something to run away from. It's our last leg of love. It's all about love, and yes, it fucking hurts. I can't change that. I don't want to change that. To change that would be to not feel, not live fully, to be numb. I spent some time being numb, and I would much rather feel my life. Grief has taught me more about love than I ever knew was possible.

"Love Is"
—Kathie Powell

Love is in the corners of our souls
Love is in a smile
Love is in tears

Love is laughing when no noise comes out
Love is fighting and making up
Love is a whisper
Love is hard
Love is easy
Love is real
Love is keeping the door open for your grown children
Love is being there when your grandchildren are born
Love is loud family dinners
Love is holding on when it seems pointless
Love is believing in forever
Love is in each breath
Love is slow dancing in the kitchen
Love is holding hands when your mad
Love is kissing anywhere
Love is saying I love you without words
Love is knowing when to be quiet
Love is painful
Love is saying goodbye when all you want to do is hold on tight and never let go
Love is letting someone be selfish
Love is not a burden
Love is loving someone till their last breath
Love is endless
Love is you

"This is love"

Chapter 6
Fear and Grief

Finding My Footing

I'm Afraid
by Kathie Powell

I'm afraid of everything
I'm afraid of losing you again
I'm afraid of being alone
I'm afraid I can't do this
I'm afraid to ask for help
I'm afraid of forgetting how you loved me

I'm afraid of everything
I'm afraid of forgetting how your voice sounded, your laugh and how you smelt
I'm afraid of who I'm becoming
I'm afraid of her
I'm afraid I'm no longer me
I'm afraid we are no longer we

I'm afraid I won't find my way back to her
I'm afraid if I find her I will lose you

I'm afraid of everything
I'm afraid there is no eternity
I'm afraid you won't come back for me
I'm afraid you won't catch me when I fall
Dear Lord, I'm afraid of everything

but . . .

In the midst of my fear, I hear your voice so very near
"I am with you, let go of fear.
Take a step into the darkness, leap, my love, don't be afraid
You are braver than you know
It's time to spread those wings and be free," you say

I answer
"Free from you? Free from this anguish?
I'm afraid to be free. I'm afraid of losing you again."

You answer
"No, my love, you are free to be you and you will never lose me. Let your fear be your fuel. Now fly, I'm right here, so let's go. I want to enjoy the ride."

I'm not so afraid anymore.

Chapter 6

For a very long time after John died, I struggled to find my footing. I was scared and lost. My true north was gone. I had no sense of direction. The above poem I wrote describes how afraid I was. I was afraid of everything.

Another Little Miracle

I was at a Christmas event at a store in mid-December when I saw a huge piece of wall art with the poem "Fear" by Kahlil Gibran, which uses a river flowing into the ocean as a metaphor for the way we experience fear and how facing it can carry us through to who we really are. I had to gulp down my tears because I was in a room full of people. The truth was that for the first time in a year, I felt seen. Fear was what I had been living in since John died.

It meant so much to me, I wanted to buy it. The woman who owned the store admitted that it had been ordered by mistake and gladly sold it to me. Funny that this large piece of art, which the shop owner considered a mistake, was not a mistake for me; it was a message. I read it over and over that evening, holding the tears back. I knew it was for me. A message that I needed. The message was that I was still here; I hadn't disappeared into my grief. As Gibran writes, "It's not about disappearing into the ocean, but of becoming the ocean." (If you're curious and want to read this poem, I encourage you to look it up online.)

The poem made me see that I'm actually not afraid anymore. I now have it hanging on a huge wall in my house at the bottom of my stairs so it's the first thing I see when I come downstairs each morning. It reminds me that even though in the beginning, my grief seemed too big to carry into my life, I learned that I can adjust to the weight of it. My grief isn't separate from who I am; it's part of me forever. Like the way a river becomes part of the ocean but doesn't disappear into it, my grief becomes a part of who I am but I don't disappear into it.

My Story of Fear

After John died and everyone had gone home and back to their lives, as they should, I sat alone in my house with Wendel, who seemed more anxious and barked at anything that moved. It scared me. I was more anxious—more anxious than I had ever been in my life.

The truth is, I was afraid. I didn't feel safe in my own home. I didn't like that people could see in my windows. I didn't feel like my doors were strong enough to keep anyone out. I felt like someone was watching me all the time, and not in a good way. I didn't go out at night. Coming home was terribly hard but more so at night. Darkness was a very scary place for me.

I had never lived on my own. I had left home when I was eighteen and moved in with my sister, then John. Suddenly, here I was, alone.

At night before going to bed, I would close everything down. Shut the shutters, close the blinds, and lock the doors.

I needed more window coverings, bigger locks, more security. My heart would race as soon as it got dark. Then I would head to bed and bring Wendel into the room and lock the door. It was a ritual I did every night with tears streaming down my face. I felt helpless to stop the fear. It was getting so big. Some nights, the weight of the fear made it hard to catch my breath. I wanted my life back. I wanted to feel safe again, but I just couldn't find my footing. The ground was very uneven. I kept stumbling into fear. Fear of what? Fear of being alone, fear of change, fear of failing . . . all of it and more. I had become a shell of myself.

God bless my grandchildren because they didn't want me to stay by myself, so I had a lot of sleepovers. Yes, I did lock the house down when they slept over. I think I passed some of my fear onto them, which I didn't mean to. Actions speak louder than words. They were so sweet, hugging and snuggling me. Letting me know we were safe together, and Wendel would protect us.

Who was I now? This scared woman who was afraid inside and outside her home? I didn't feel safe with her either. Everything was up to me now, someone I had never trusted. Fuck.

So I set to working on getting my house to feel safer and safer. The first thing I did was to get my doors upgraded. I installed window coverings for shutting out the world but still letting in the light.

Gradually, before I even realised what was happening, Wendel and I went to bed, and I left the bedroom door open and unlocked. I remember sitting up in bed and realising the door was open. I sat there, waiting. I could hear my breath. I talked myself into laying back and told myself I was okay, that I was safe, and then I fell asleep. I think I slept through the night. It was a big step, and I made it through.

Maybe part of it was that the room was different now. It was my room. There was joy in the room now; it wasn't dark and scary. This room still held his memory but not the pain. I could breathe again in our room, in my room. It was going to be okay.

The fear of going to bed at night didn't just disappear, but I learned to acknowledge it. In the beginning, I had many conversations in my head about what was real and not so I could settle down for the night.

Fear crept into my life in many unwelcome ways. Fear undid me, but it also brought back the fight in me. I had so much fear. The fear of breaking down in front of others. Let me tell you, that fear was justified, because it happened a lot. Grief makes people uncomfortable. I think I was afraid of being the cause of discomfort. I remember I cried, talking to my neighbours, who quickly walked the other way, not knowing what to say or do. It was only slightly awkward. I've cried in the grocery store, at the doctor's office, in the bank, in coffee shops, and during a workout. I've cried watching a grandchild's sports game. And the list goes on.

I was afraid of making the wrong decisions, of which I have made many, and I'm still here. I was afraid of being a

Chapter 6

burden because there was so much I didn't know how to do. But I learned a lot of new skills, and I learned that it's okay to ask for help from time to time. Mostly I was afraid of never being me again. I know I'm different, and I will never return to the me I was before John died, but I fought hard to come to accept who I was meant to be. She isn't the same, but I like her. She is more independent, she is learning to trust herself and others, she is fun, and she is loving. The reality is that we won't be the same after losing someone we love so deeply. Part of us is missing.

This next part of the journey is all about self-discovery.

The things I know now . . . I've learned a lot this past year. Mostly, I've learned to show myself grace in the midst of this experience. My heart is to share what I know and get people talking about grief, dying, and death—things each one of us who lives and who loves will experience at one point or another. There is so much fear regarding these topics, because we don't talk about them or learn about them. It's become my mission to open the conversation to help us all let go of fear and embrace our lives fully and live till we die.

My last fear, one I can say I've overcome, was the fear of Tuesdays. Each week I would fixate on the trauma of John's last moments, his last breath, see the people taking his body out the front door on a gurney and in a body bag. These vivid memories made Tuesday hard to bear.

But . . .

I have now reframed my thinking of Tuesday. I decided to look up the day of the week John was born, and it was on a Tuesday!

Tuesday gave me the gift of John. Tuesday, you gave me one last morning with my love. Tuesday, you gave me more conversation with him. Tuesday, you gave me one more time to hear his perspective on life and hard things. Tuesday, you let me hear him say, "I love you" one more time. Tuesday, you gave me just a little more time to love him and be loved by him. Tuesday, you let him decide it was time to go. Tuesday, you gave him freedom from his pain. Tuesday, you allowed me to fulfil my promise, to hold his hand when he took his last breath. Tuesday, I didn't realise how very kind you were.

From now on, I will let Tuesday bring what it brings to me and feel it without judgement.

Chapter 7
Going through His Things

It's Not "Just Stuff"

Like so many things in grief, there is no right way or wrong way to approach sorting through a loved one's belongings after a death. But one thing I found for me was I needed to make a plan. I'm a planner.

Soon after he died, even before the celebration of life, I let my children and grandchildren go through the things they wanted out of his clothes. This process was kind of beautiful as I watched them go through and pick things out that brought up a memory that was special to them. Now I love seeing John's children and grandkids wear some things he used to wear. It doesn't hurt like I thought it would. It still makes me smile when I see his things being worn by his loved ones; it's like a little piece of him shows up for me.

But I didn't move onto the next phase for a while.

In March, I had to sort out our taxes and go through more of his things. Things I had never done before. This overwhelming process brought me to the knowledge that it was time to move on to his clothes. John wanted all his clothes donated to a thrift store that supports one of his causes. A place that gives back the net proceeds to helping others in need. He wanted all his military things given to Aaron. He told me where to look. I remember him saying, "I want Aaron to understand what kind of soldier I was." This was very important to him.

I went through his things in stages. First, I took everything out of the closet and dresser and thought, "Holy man, how many suit jackets does one guy need?" Then I checked myself and thought, "Wait till someone goes through my closet." But he really did have a lot of jackets and boots. He didn't purge his closet like I did annually. In this process, I found out that John was a very sentimental man. I was shocked by the things he kept. I didn't know. He kept things that were important little keepsakes to him. He really was romantic. It was all so heartbreaking. How many times can a heart break?

I laid things out on the bed and put things in piles. I stood there and looked at everything and felt like I might throw up. Then I lay on top of all his clothes and I sobbed; this sound came out of me that I didn't recognise. It was a guttural cry. It was all too much at that moment. The taxes, the house, the yard, the finances, his clothes, and going through all his things. It felt like I was being gutted. I felt like I was erasing him. I froze more times than I moved.

Chapter 7

Before John died, I found a letter I wrote him when I was nineteen years old. Every sentiment in the letter was still true at sixty-two years old. The letter was in a file I found looking for something else. It caught me by surprise because I didn't know he had kept it. We had moved so many times. It never got lost. I went upstairs and read it out loud to him and cried. He said, "Of course I kept it. It's beautiful; this was our beginning. I love you." I thought, "Oh my God, there is still so much I need to know about you. How am I only finding this out now?" I put it back away and then found it again later as I was organising things. Instant tears.

I am grateful I found these sweet keepsakes that I had given him because they reinforced what I already knew. I was loved wholly and completely by this man, and he knew that he was loved wholly and completely by me.

I know things are just things, but these things he touched, wore, saved, and picked out. The ache I felt is indescribable to most people. I felt exhausted, fragile, like I couldn't stand up. I felt so lost as I hugged one of the T-shirts into my face. "I don't want to do this." I sobbed and lay back onto his things and fell asleep. I wasn't ready.

It took me another month to donate them. Remember your grief, your journey. No one can tell you that you have to get rid of their stuff. It's not their decision; it's yours and in your time.

What did I keep? The running shoes he wore to the hospital. They are in the closet in the spare bedroom. The

The Hardest, Not the Worst Year

T-shirt he wore to the hospital—it's under my pillow. The sweatshirt and socks he wore are in my bedside table. I used to hug the T-shirt each night; now it's safely under my head. The other things I'm not ready to part with, and they can stay right where they are. I kept his wedding bands, his glasses, wallet, and some ID I didn't have to give back to the government. I have his ashes with a bunch of little things inside referenced in chapter 4. All these things hold moments in time for me, and I cherish them. Some days I don't touch them, and other days I hold them and reminisce about our journey. Some days I cry, and others I don't. But every day I feel. The ashes stay here with me until it's my time to transition from life to death. We will be together in ashes and together in spirit one day. Till then, I will hold onto the things I need to help me through.

I have kept the things I just can't part with, and so have the kids and grandkids . . . we all have something, but more importantly, we all have him in our hearts forever. That's what matters most.

Going through the things of someone you love after they die is hard. It hurts and it brings up a lot for some, and for others it can be a cathartic experience. Again, this whole journey through grief is unique to you, as is how you need to process and work through this part. Here are some things I did that I thought I would share . . . not in a way to tell you what to do; it's just a frame of reference so that when you are starting your process, you have something to work from (or not).

When you feel you are ready to start, these are the five categories I found it helpful to sort John's things into:

- Save for you: The things you can't let go of yet
- Save for others: Things for family and friends
- Sell: Things that are in excellent condition you might want to sell or consign
- Donate: Things that are in good condition
- Textile recycling: A place for those things too worn to donate or keep

Ask for help if you need to, or do it on your own . . . it is your experience, and you need to do what works for you. Be kind to yourself, and remember it might be tempting to want to do it all at once, but taking breaks is important because it can be too overwhelming.

Every one of us walks this journey of loss differently. Some of us hold onto things for years, and others let go of things quicker. Neither is wrong; it's your process. Regardless of when, it will hurt, and it's hard. So give yourself grace to do things in your own way and own time.

Give yourself grace as you navigate your loss . . . this is not a straight line. One person's experience might not be your road map, but it might give you some insight as you walk through knowing it's okay to do it your way.

I know nothing will bring back the people we have lost. I get it so much more now. Things are just that—things—

but memories hold love and moments. They can keep the memories alive within us. Something John always said was, "Stuff doesn't matter. It's nice, but it's not what's most important. Love is. We are. That's what's important."

I get that, but I still need some stuff to hold onto, babe.

Going through a loved one's things can be a devastating process. You may stumble upon objects you haven't seen in a long time. You are touching the things they wore; it's a continuous reminder of the person you've lost. It can be really painful. Go at your own pace here. Do it when it feels right for you. Your process won't look exactly like mine. Honour your process; there is no timeline to get this done. The truth is that you don't have to do anything. Your grief, your love, your process. No one but you can tell you when "it's time."

So you might think I have gone through all of John's things, and it's all done. I can't say that, because there is an area in the basement that I have been saying I am going to go through for at least nine months now. Every time I go to do it, I stop. I'm just not ready—not ready for the pain of seeing his handwriting, finding pictures, going through all the paperwork of our life together. I have stopped beating myself up for this because it's a process, and it's mine. It's not time yet.

Chapter 8
Jack's Moment

Part of Healing Is Working through the Hard Stuff

Recently my granddaughter started to ask me, "Grandma, one day when you are in the hospital . . . " She stopped, looked at me, and then softly said, "But you won't die there. Can I come see you?"

I smiled at her; I could hear her concern. "Nora," I said, "I hope I don't die in the hospital. I want to come home. And of course, you can come see me, if you want to, but if you don't, it's okay too. Whatever you feel you need when we get there one day. You are feeling a little anxious because you didn't get to see Papa, aren't you?"

She nodded. "Only Jack got to see him."

Four out of seven of our grandchildren live with the fact that they didn't get to see their papa those last few days. The youngest two don't really have that sense of loss, but each of the others do. It's been something we've talked about a lot since John died. They were so confused. Why didn't he want to see them? Didn't he love them?

Jack's Moment

John had been home for only three days, and he was getting more and more tired with each passing day. He slept more. He didn't eat much, if anything, and only drank pink Gatorade. I often wonder if we asked him what he liked or if he just took what we gave him.

John had decided he did not want to see his grandchildren. He didn't want to hurt them or cause them any more pain. The thing in all of this is that you can't keep them safe from the pain of losing someone they love; you can't shield them from it. Also, it was too painful for him to see them seeing him in the condition he was in. I struggled to understand but honoured his wishes until Sunday night.

My girls and I talked about Jack seeing his papa. Jack is our oldest; he was fourteen years old at the time and six feet tall. John and Jack had a special first-grandchild bond. It was often said they were soulmates. Jack taught John how to be a good papa, which he would have to share one day with six others who each became a soulmate to their papa in their own unique way.

John was born to be a father, and the icing on the cake was being a papa. He was such a devoted papa. From reading stories, to playing with monster trucks, Hot Wheels, trains, and LEGO, and playing in the sandbox, he was all in. John was always on the floor with him, with all of them. He played with them, read to them, coloured with them, snuggled, and watched silly kids' shows, and he showered them with love. I cooked with them, snuggled them, took them shopping, coloured, and loved them too. Our love wasn't something to compare, but we connected differently. We were a good team.

On Christmas morning, Sarah's kids saw him. It was a short visit; he wasn't well. Everyone got a hug, and we went home. Rayna's family was sick, and Jill's family was out of town, so those grandkids missed seeing him. I think we may have FaceTimed, but I can't remember. Levi saw him the morning everything changed; he had slept over the night before. Papa was not very present because he didn't feel well, but he did have a few jokes, and they said their "I love yous" when I took Levi out for breakfast.

Then everything changed. Papa was in the hospital, and no one got to see him. They sent pictures with handwritten notes of love. Things to remind him he was a very loved papa.

I asked John if the grandkids could come see him. He looked at me with concern and said, "No, I don't want them to see me like this in here. This is no place for children. It will be too hard."

All I could think was how much they loved him and he loved them. I didn't agree, and I didn't understand. I never asked him to share his fears about anything or whether he had any. I wish I had, because I think I would have uncovered a fear he had from his childhood: a ten-year-old boy who spent time in and out of the hospital because his father was very ill and died in a hospital. I do remember him saying one day on one of our walks through the halls in the hospital that he hated hospitals and the smell of them ever since he was little. He didn't want to put that on his grandchildren.

Now back to Sunday. I told Sarah to bring Jack to see his papa. I felt it was so important for Jack to see him and for John to see Jack. I felt like it was important for them to be able to say something to each other. One moment for each of them. I didn't romanticise it, but I didn't envision what they would experience.

Jack's Story from His Mom's, Sarah's, Perspective:

We drove up to your house. Our ride over was mostly silent, neither of us knowing what to say. I'm sure I said a few things to reassure him, but it's a bit of a blur. When we got inside, we went upstairs to your bedroom. You came up with us—it had been over a month since Jack had been there, and Dad was all set up in the dining room.

Upstairs, you spoke to him and told him what to expect when he saw Papa, both of us trying to protect him, even though nothing we could say would be enough to prepare or protect him.

When it was time to go, we walked downstairs. Jack, then me, then you . . . I think. I remember you saying as we walked down, "He doesn't know Jack is here—I didn't tell him" or something to that effect. My heart sank; I was scared.

You went in first to tell him someone was here to see him. Jack walked in, and I came in behind him. Jack turned and faced

Dad and just broke down. He fell to his knees. They were holding hands, and Dad just had his eyes closed, like it was too painful to look. It was. The heartbreak in that room was palpable—we all felt it. Jack hugged him and left the dining room. I followed, but Dad looked at me and said, "Thank you, thank you," and I went out and held my six-foot-tall son while he wailed.

I took him upstairs, thinking this was the worst thing I could have ever done to him—just broke his heart into pieces, traumatised him forever. He kept telling me it was okay, that he loved me and he loved Papa so much. But he was crying so hard, I didn't think he'd ever be able to stop.

Afterward, he went out for a walk with you or Maggie; I can't remember exactly. I took him home. We hugged. We cried. I don't remember much else after that.

You can hear the trauma in this moment and also feel the love. My decision.

I FaceTimed Jack to ask if it was okay to talk about that night, and he said, "Yes, it's okay, Grandma."

Sunday Night from Jack's Perspective

I remember starting our conversation with, "Remember that one night Papa was still in the hospital and you looked at me and said, 'Papa is going to be okay, right? You had cancer and you got better. You are cured.' And I said back to you, knowing the truth that yes, I did get better. Well, I didn't answer the question honestly or really at all. I didn't have the heart to tell you he had no hope because I wanted hope."

Jack said that yeah, he remembered.

I asked him how Sunday came to happen. Did he ask to come visit? He said his mom just asked him if he wanted to go see Papa. She did it with just him, without his brother or sister. Jack said yes, he wanted to go. I asked him how it was. He said it was a lot. He was nervous and excited to see his papa. It had been so long. He told me when he came into the room, it sucked. He was surprised by how slim Papa had gotten and by the oxygen tubes on his face.

I asked him, "Was it his eyes?" He said that no, Papa's eyes were the same. He remembered kneeling down in front of Papa holding his hand, and Papa said, "Hi, Jack. I love you." And Jack said, "I love you." Jack remembered leaving quickly and crying upstairs. He said it all became real. I asked him if he was glad he saw him. He told me that yes, he was very glad he got to see him one more time.

My Perspective

Now my account is somewhat different from a fourteen-year-old boy who was devastated, seeing his dying papa for the first and only time. I share this story so you can see within the few moments this held in our lives, how we saw it and how we felt was unique to our experience. Grief and trauma can leave our brains a bit foggy, as it's trying to protect us from what we are not ready to face yet. This part of our story is one I struggle with. I feel guilt, and I feel like it was the right thing to do for both of them.

Chapter 8

I remember getting up and vaguely talking with Jack upstairs, trying to prepare him for what he was about to see. I did my best. Then we went downstairs, and I admitted to Sarah I didn't tell her father because I didn't want him to say no. I just remember the look on her face, one of "What?" But we kept right on walking towards his room. The curtains were partially closed, and John was sitting in his chair, watching TV.

I walked in first and said, "There is someone here I think you are going to want to see." His face changed, and he looked shocked and concerned. Then Jack walked in. This tall, slender boy walked into this small room that held his papa. John looked surprised to see Jack, and I remember hearing him say, "Hi, Jack," and Jack saying, "Hi, Papa," as he knelt down in front of his papa, holding his hand.

John first said, "I love you, Jack."

And Jack said, "I love you, Papa," through gulps of sobs they came from deep within him. Jack got up, and Sarah took hold of him, and they left the room. We could still hear Jack's sobs. I believe this is the very first time I heard the sound of anguish. The sound that comes from deep within your soul, an ache that cries out without remorse, only pain. We all felt it.

John looked at me. "How could you do this? How could you do this to him?"

His face said it all. This is what he wanted to protect them all from, the pain of losing him.

I took a deep breath and said boldly, "This is love, what you talk about all the time. This boy has loved you his whole life, and he is about to lose you. You can't protect him from that."

I felt so guilty that I had caused them both—well, all of us—this kind of pain. But the truth is, I didn't cause it. This was love, and this was loss and grief.

To this day, my heart breaks at the thought of this moment, but I can't change it. Would I if I could? All I know is what my heart wanted for both of them, and somewhere in the midst of all this, I think there was a sweet moment when they both felt the pain of loss and the power of love.

I don't remember much after that except going to check on Jack and hold him. He looked at me and said, "Grandma, I am glad I got to see him." I cried, and I said, "Me too."

When I came back to the room, John looked at me as I said I was so sorry but I felt it was the right thing to do. I honestly don't remember what he said, if he said anything. I held him and didn't want to let him go. I wish I could have protected his heart from the pain of losing all of us.

I sat across from him, and he said to me, "Kath, you have to promise me to tell me what is happening. No more surprises. I don't know what's going on day to day. Who is coming and going. Please tell me what to expect each day. I need to know. I have no control over anything anymore." I promised him I would not surprise him with anything or anyone. I would tell him everything. So for the next two days, I shared with him everything that was happening.

Chapter 8

I found out that my husband, who was a man who asked for little and was very self-sufficient, felt very vulnerable and also had, in that one moment, lost trust in me. I think that is what hurt the most. I broke his trust. I did something I felt was for his own good without his consent. "The road to hell is paved with good intentions," as the proverb by Abbot Saint Bernard of Clairvaux says.

My actions caused pain instead of the good intentions that led me to choose to do this. I had no idea what to expect. I could not predict any of it. I just wanted closure for them, but you cannot create closure for someone else. I could not make it better. Now some will say it was the right thing because Jack is glad he got to see him. I can't answer for John because he didn't express anything to me besides, "How could you have done this?" I know he forgave me. Now I need to forgive myself. The only solace I have is that he thanked Sarah. I believe even with John's fragile, broken heart, he was grateful to see Jack one last time. Again, I hear my justification for this act of love that hurt the man I love more than anything in this world.

Part of healing is working through the hard stuff, being courageous enough to be vulnerable. Brave enough to be honest. The key to healing is being truthful about your responsibility, your part. What you saw, felt, heard, and did. Forgiving myself is the hard stuff that will take more courage than I think I have and the vulnerability to admit I made a mistake in not telling him and honouring that fact that I did the right thing letting Jack come to see him. But in doing so, it caused John unfair pain because he couldn't prepare even a little bit emotionally. It's not an easy mistake to come to terms with.

Would I do it again? Only if I told him first. My heart didn't trust him enough to say yes. I never gave him the opportunity to make the decision; this is my regret. Note I said *regret*, because I let go of the guilt, knowing I never meant to hurt either of them.

Something I will share with you in case you are feeling any guilt for a decision you made in your grief, in your pain, in your love:

Forgive yourself.

For the decisions you made with your heart and not your head.

For lacking the foresight to see this would hurt them and you.

For wanting to be right.

For trying to make everyone feel better and believing you could.

For being human.

Love is not the absence of hurting someone. Love is getting through the mistakes, the hurts, and the disappointments and loving each other through it all. Real, messy love is a statement to the depth of our emotional connections and the resilience of the human spirit.

This was a hard lesson and one I really didn't get to discuss with John as to the lengths we would normally go through when there was a bump in the road, a misstep, and a hurt. We would sit and work through it, listening to each other. It didn't happen. Neither of us had the strength. We got through it with love.

After going through this whole year, feeling such guilt, I wish I could hold the woman I was, be there with her, and tell her all the things I know now. Tell her she did a really good job. Tell her I get why she did what she did. And thank her for taking responsibility. Now it's time to forgive.

Love doesn't protect us from pain, because pain is a part of love. This moment, Jack's moment, was all about love.

"Jack"

Chapter 9
He Asked for Little

I Promised to Support and Stand by You . . .

As John's strength waned during his weeks in the hospital, each passing day seemed to weigh heavier upon him. He wasn't one to demand much, but when he did, it held significance. At the time, I was still deeply involved in my work with grief clients, nearing the end of our journey together.

John and I had our routine while he was in the hospital; it involved exchanging texts every morning and evening. While my messages tended to be lengthy, John's were short yet filled with meaning. Sleep eluded me those days. I was often awake before 4:00 a.m., and our text exchanges began early.

On January 11, with a scheduled call with a client for a follow-up, I informed John I would be a bit later, promising to be there by 11:00 a.m. and would be staying until he drifted off to sleep for the night, a ritual he always adhered to, insisting I return home after supper. His response to my message shocked me. This wasn't like him, ever.

"I really wish you could postpone this client. Just wanted you to know how I feel."

His words cut through me. How could I prioritise someone else over him at this moment? What was wrong with me? I felt a wave of sickness wash over me, torn by conflicting emotions. Grief demands to be acknowledged and worked through, and this individual had put in the effort; all I needed to do was check in. Truth be told, I could have easily rescheduled—my clients would have understood. They did. Perhaps it was my subconscious way of briefly escaping from my own life, sitting with them in their grief. I could detach myself for an hour.

Without hesitation, I replied, assuring John I would be there immediately. His subsequent message, "I want/I need you," made me realise how hard this was for him. I just wanted to hold him and reassure him. I responded, "I want and need you, too, more than I can ever express." It felt as though an immense weight was slowly crushing me, an unbearable pressure, like having my heart squeezed. Was this the sensation of heartbreak?

Arriving at the hospital, I found John waiting, he looked as beautiful as ever, even though he was visibly more tired. I hugged him, saying I was sorry, but he simply reassured me, "You're so good to your clients, and I understand that. But right now, I really need you. No need to apologise." Tears flowed freely from both our eyes, the weight of our limited time together pressed down on us; the exact measure of how short our time was, we didn't know. Yet the depth of our mutual need for one another remained tangible, whether in moments of his rest or my constant nervous chatter, seeking to drown out my own pain. I felt like I was suffocating under the weight of losing him.

It was a trying day for John. He had one more request, a touching request. "Kath, I need you to find my old friend. I want to thank him." Without hesitation, I agreed. Then I asked him how. John already knew the answer, instructing me to reach out to specific individuals, confident that if anyone could provide the information, it would be one of them.

So my search began, trying to locate John's long-lost friend. With the help of the person I contacted, a PPCLI group on Facebook swiftly tracked down the friend. I provided my contact information, and a few days later, he called.

The room was dark, whether from the gloomy weather or drawn curtains, John resting quietly, his sleep growing more frequent. I vividly recall the moment my phone rang, displaying an unfamiliar Winnipeg number. I didn't answer. Then I realised it was his friend. I quickly listened to the voice mail; it was him. I returned the call immediately, the fear of missing our opportunity undeniable. Despite initial missed connections, we finally connected, and I answered.

Initiating the conversation, I expressed gratitude for his call, then switched to speakerphone so he and John could talk. Though separated by over three decades, their connection felt timeless. John sought to express his profound gratitude and the deep-rooted impact his friend had on his life. Tears welled in my eyes as I listened to them share stories, their mutual appreciation evident in every word exchanged. Though the words "I love you" were left unspoken, their sentiment lingered in the air, hanging heavy with emotion.

It was their final conversation, a moment of bittersweet beauty made possible by each individual who played a part, but most notably by the friend who reached out to bid farewell. John cherished his friendships, particularly those made during his time in the military. He entrusted me with the task of sharing his thoughts of appreciation to another friend via email, a task he grew too weak to complete. This friend was even more important to John, and I think he wanted an email so the emotional toll would be less. Thankfully, I had the opportunity to meet with his friend at John's celebration of life, where I shared John's deep love and appreciation for their friendship, a sentiment echoed by many other soldiers who attended.

Before his passing, a special young man, our nephew, made a touching visit, offering his support and affection to his uncle. Their bond was indescribable yet evident, filled with a unique blend of love and lighthearted teasing. Though I didn't overhear their conversations, I could sense their significance, knowing they exchanged the words they each needed to hear. When I look at our nephew today, I see traces of John, but mostly, I see a remarkable individual shaped by his parents, some of his uncle's influence, but mostly shaped by himself.

Chapter 9

Shortly after my nephew's departure, John passed away. I am immensely grateful he made the journey, not just for us, but also for himself and John.

This experience taught me a valuable lesson: it's crucial to express gratitude and love to those who positively impact our lives before it's too late, for tomorrow is never guaranteed. Our time is finite, and every moment counts. So if you find yourself missing someone or longing to reconnect, don't hesitate to reach out—a simple text message could brighten their day. After all, it's never too late, until it is, as time waits for no one.

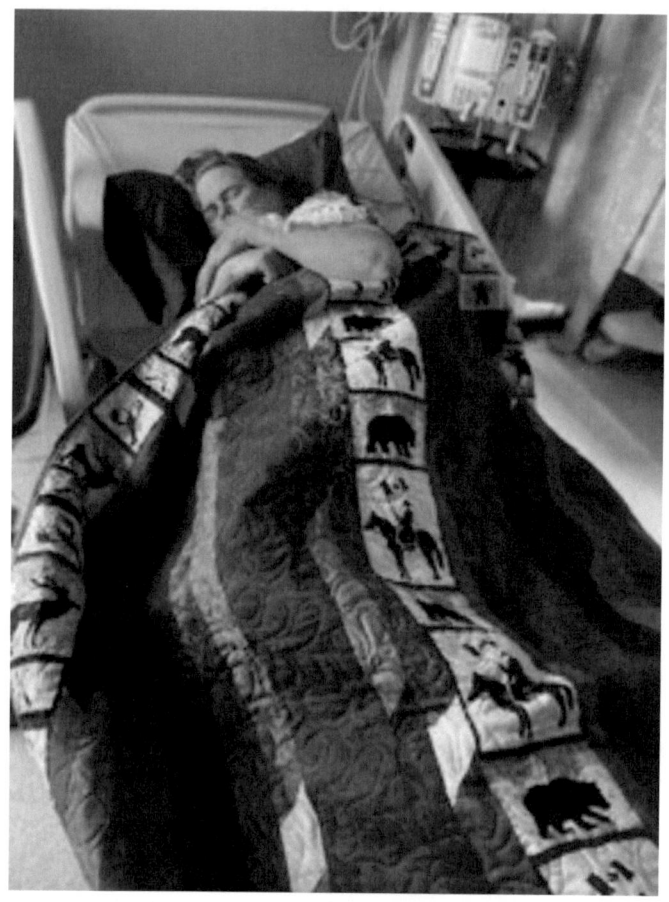

"The Quilt of Valour"
This was presented to John January 13th hand made with love and respect by a woman named Diane – It symbolizes gratitude for his military service.

Chapter 10

Signs

11:11, Crows and Tattoos

After a loved one dies we search for signs of them. Our brains are trying to navigate this devastating change.

After John died, I often wondered why I was the person who didn't get the messages or signs from above. I started thinking maybe my faith wasn't strong enough, or maybe I didn't deserve to hear from him. Maybe I'd done something wrong.

When I hear of others finding signs, having dreams, or feeling their loved one's presence near them, I am jealous. Jealous that they get to connect one more time and I don't.

Are the only things I have left of him memories and the pain to hold onto?

In those early days, I needed more.

I went on a search to find someone who could bring me to John. A medium. Someone who would connect us. Someone who would feel his presence and tell me how I could feel him nearby. Someone John could speak through. So I went on the hunt. I found someone who had great reviews and had been in the medium/psychoanalysis/mystic business for over forty years. I was sceptical but still wanted to believe it was possible to talk with him or feel his presence or have him give me a sign he was near.

I booked a meeting and paid my money, and we met on FaceTime. She was a bit older than I, sweet and kind, and she dove right into my loss quickly. Now if you follow me on social media, you know I'm an open book. But there are some parts I don't share, and no one knows except John and me. I felt like she wouldn't have a hard time telling me things she thought I needed to hear if she had gone through my social media accounts. I tried not to let my open book cloud my acceptance of what she would bring to me. In this meeting with her, in this meeting with him. She told me things that she could have read about us on social media...but maybe she really could have connected with him and shared her honest experience. I won't know for sure till John and I meet again and he can tell me face to face. But . . . she did have some insight and signs that he was present. She told me things only we would know. He was letting me know he was with us. That unsettled me. I wasn't afraid; I was just unprepared for someone we didn't know to share things they had no way of knowing.

Hmm . . .

We spoke for an hour, and I got to ask him some questions, which felt weird because I wasn't sure how to ask

Chapter 10

him . . . should I do it through her or just talk to him myself? To be honest, I felt awkward, afraid, and shy. So I went through her; it felt like the right thing to do. If he really was there, I know he was laughing at me but also thinking of a way to make sure I knew he was there.

Before I spoke, I had to take a few deep breaths because I was afraid of what he would say, if he was there, regarding some of my questions. I didn't want to cry. I was afraid that I hadn't done enough for him. I was afraid I had messed up. I was afraid I had disappointed him in the end. In the middle of my questions, she looked at me and told me sweetly, "He says you made the right decision and to stop beating yourself up for it." He told her I did the right thing, and he thanked me for having the courage to do it. He told her we gave him the best care. He felt safe and loved till he took his last breath. He told her to tell me I was on the right path and I need to keep doing the work. He told her he was proud of me.

I wept. I could hardly compose myself. I wanted to believe everything she was saying. I needed to believe everything she was saying.

She never said what exactly he was referring to when he said I did the right thing, but I knew, and I so desperately needed to hear what he said through her.

I don't know if what she said was some generic line mediums used in general terms for those of us left with things we wished had been resolved and made clearer to all of us before our loved ones die so we don't hold onto that guilt, regret, or pain. Regardless of what the truth is, I will hold onto that moment and his words. I know he knew how very much I loved him and that I would do anything for him. He knew he was loved when he took his last breath and left this earth. That I can hold onto and live with.

She told me I knew deep down when he was with me and not to question if a sign or feeling happened. If I thought it was him, to believe it, because it *was* him. Now because of this encounter, I've found I have had a few of those moments where I felt his presence. Ones I had dismissed. The clearest one was just after he died (if you know, you know). I truly believe he was letting us know he was okay. It was a clear sign to me at the time. I remember I laughed and said out loud, "He's letting us know he is okay." She told me that that was exactly what he was doing.

I see this number sequence 11:11 all the time. I see it on my phone, my watch, on TV, at games, and many other places. I think this might be a thing, and it became apparent yesterday when Rayna shared the time she was leaving the hospital ward after her emergency surgery . . . it was 11:11. I believe it was a sign he was there watching over her and making sure she was okay.

As I write this, tears are streaming down my face. There are days when I am angry and frustrated in this process of life without John and living with a grief that is gutting me.

Grief, I am now very acquainted with your company. I understand you go hand-in-hand with the love I have for him,

Chapter 10

so I embrace you, and I hate you. I understand your worth and your presence in my life. Grief, you undo me time and time again. Just when I think I'm okay, the floor drops out, and I'm on my knees, unable to catch my breath.

Searching for John in the great beyond alone was defeating. I miss him more than words can say. The most vital part of me is gone. The anguish I feel every day is real, as real as the love I hold for John each and every day. So maybe, just maybe, I do feel him. I just needed to open my mind and heart to it and feel his messages from heaven for me.

My granddaughter Nora always tells me Papa is here with us. She'll say, "Grandma, he is right there. See?" She looks up at the sky and blows him kisses and gives him the finger (it's something he started, and she does it all the time now). I am sure he laughs every time she does it and sends one right back to her full of love and silliness.

The funny thing is John was very logical and this would not be his thing, but he knew me better than anyone. If he could and it were possible, he would use whatever means available to let me know that he loves me and he is watching over all of us. That he is with us, deep within each one of our hearts. I'm feeling less defeated in our connection, hopeful. I'm listening a little more intently, and I'm open to feeling his presence if any of this is possible.

I want to tell you about my crow. Shortly after John died and spring had come into the air, I noticed a crow on our walks. It wasn't like before; it was one in particular. This crow was watching me. It unsettled Wendel at first, but then we both got used to our encounters. I looked forward to it. I would often shout out, "Good morning, Mr. Crow!" And then quietly, "Is that you, John?" This crow became a constant for us on our walks, and I looked forward to meeting with him and sometimes his partners, but he was mostly alone. I felt our connection.

I decided to research crows and their relationships and grief. Crows are known to form strong pair bonds, often mating for life. They display remarkable loyalty and dedication to their partners. They work together to build nests, raise their young, and protect their territory. While not all crow pairs necessarily stay together for life, many do exhibit this behaviour, forging relationships that endure the test of time. I also found out that when a crow loses its partner, it can experience grief and sadness, much like humans do. The surviving crow may display behaviours indicative of mourning, such as calling out repeatedly, searching for their mate, or remaining near the place where their partner passed away. Some crows may even refuse to leave the side of their deceased mate for a period of time. Crows are social creatures, and they often form strong connections with other members of their flock, which can provide comfort and support during times of loss. Maybe John comes to visit me within this crow? Maybe he is letting me know he is always with me? Maybe it's just a crow?

Once on our walk, we heard a loud cawing. It was relentless. It wouldn't stop. I hadn't seen our crow that

Chapter 10

morning but was preoccupied with something else and didn't pay any attention until the noise got very close. I turned around and about twenty-five feet away from us was a lone coyote. I gasped. I remember John telling me it wasn't safe to walk in the wooded areas early in the morning because of coyotes. But I wasn't in the trees; I was on the outskirts. I held my breath. I looked up, and in the tree above the coyote was the crow. He had been trying to get my attention, and he got it. We were right by the fenced dog park, and no dogs were inside it, so I quickly took Wendel into the enclosure. I didn't know what else to do. We waited, and funnily enough, Wendel never noticed the coyote. That coyote stared at me for what felt like a very long time. The crow stayed close. Wendel just kept sniffing, and I kept watching and praying we were safe. Then the coyote took one last look and went into the woods. I stayed still, waiting for some time. Then I shouted to the crow, "Thank you for saving us!" And I quickly left that dog park, and this old gal ran home.

Was the crow John or the coyote? Or was it all just a coincidence?

On March 28 I went in and got a tattoo of 11:11 on my arm. The same arm with the words reading, "I love you" with a spade tattooed. Also above that I got one more little tattoo of two crows—one on a line and one flying back to the line. It's a symbol of us. Currently, I'm on the line alone until the day he comes to bring me with him to our new home in eternity.

The Hardest, Not the Worst Year

My tattoos were always a thing for me. I got things I liked. A few have more meaning, and others are just fun, no stories. I have one on my shoulder with his name. I got it for him. It reads, "John Peter, I love you not just for who you are, but for who I am when I'm with you," a quote by Elizabeth Barrett Browning. He loved it and was so proud that I put his name on my body. Then after he died, I got another, larger tattoo representing him, my children, and my grandchildren. He is the arrow. He was always the one who found the way; I was never lost when I was with him. I cherish these signs and symbols of our story.

I don't know where you are in this journey, but I want you to know that however you are grieving is exactly your right way. No one can tell you whether it's right or wrong. No one can tell you how to feel. No one can tell you not to cry or that you don't cry enough. No one has had your exact experience. So just know if you see or feel your loved one in numbers, feathers, pennies, dreams, kittens, dogs, birds, butterflies, or breezes, that's yours to hold onto. If you don't feel anything, there is nothing wrong with you. Remember, each one of us has their own grief story. My story right here may be in my mind's eye, but at this point, I don't care. My heart is telling me he is with me. Right now my head is listening to my heart.

"Meaningful signs and wonders"

Chapter 11
The Promise

I promise to love you forever

I promise to love you unconditionally, to cherish our bond, and to honour our commitment for as long as we both shall live.

I'm not counting the weeks anymore. The moment, the date, is etched in my mind forever.

It's been over a year since I lost you, since your children, grandchildren and friends lost you. It's been over a year since I heard you say, "I love you too."

The ache isn't less; it's just more familiar.

Grief is an interesting friend. I used to call her "she/her" because I felt like she was an extension of me, but I think it's "he/him"—he is an extension of John.

Grief, you are always there, always ready to listen and let me cry without judgement. Grief understands my pain and does not try to fix me. If I ignore grief, he waits and arrives whenever there is an opening. He isn't mad or pushy. He is honest and committed to honouring the pain of my loss. All he asks for in return is my honesty and commitment to my grief, and my love. My grief is him. My grief is John.

I get afraid sometimes that I'm going to forget something about us. That John will grow further away from me as I get more familiar with him being gone. That I will forget the real relationship and start believing in something I wished had been or in only the "good parts" of our life together. You know what? Even the hard stuff was the good part. I didn't think the hard, messy parts were good until now, but they were. They were part of the good because we always made it through. We always learned something. We grew together, closer somehow. We never forgot the *why* of us or the love we carried. We fought, we cried, and we even gave up sometimes (mostly me) but always found our way home. Our relationship was not perfect, but it was.

When John lay dying—the hardest part of our journey together—we grew even closer, and our love grew bigger and deeper. Amidst all the pain, this was the beautiful part, the gift.

I listen to videos to hear his voice and imagine him saying, "I love you" to me in them. Even when he was being silly, saying something to one of our grandchildren in a Snapchat video. I wish I had captured more moments, but you can't do that without interrupting the realness of a moment. John was the one who always wanted to be in the moment, to feel it and remember it. So now I listen to the sound of his voice and remember him saying, "I love you, Kath" in my mind. I love the sound of him saying "Kath." It was soothing and so beautiful. I love his voice. I love his laugh. I love his insight and wisdom. I love the things that used to make me mad. I miss all of him.

I am in this strange place where I am used to him not being here. I don't like it, but I know and understand the feeling of being alone. Alone, as in without him. I never minded being alone until now because I was never really alone; he was always coming home to me. This loneliness is so loud, final, and real. This alone is forever. The loneliness is longing.

What is forever? How did I mean "forever" when he was here with me? I guess my version of forever before January 24, 2023, was forever here on earth. He and I until we both died together, not one before the other. My forever was unrealistic and romantic. I think that is why in the beginning he would tell me, "Nothing is forever," and I would cry and say, "But say *we* are." John was always the logical one. But he, too, ended up believing we were forever because he believed in eternity.

Right now, my forever here on earth is grieving him. It's the longing. I still believe we are forever; we have just been given a moment in time to pause. A moment in time for me to learn what I still need to learn and for him to get accustomed to his new home in eternity, whatever that looks like. I know if we get to decorate, he is saving that for me.

Our forever will continue in eternity.

Words of promise I meditate on each morning: "John, until you reach for me when my time comes and you bring me home with you, I will miss you forever and love you into eternity. Until then, my love, I will continue your legacy of love and commitment to serving others. I will pass on stories of you to our children and grandchildren. Your legacy lives on in our love, in each story, each memory, and each person's life you touched with yours."

A little amendment to our original vows:

I promise to continue to love you unconditionally, to cherish our bond, and to honour our commitment for as long as I live. I will carry our love deep within my heart until we meet again.

Chapter 12
My Journal

The Last Twenty-Eight Days

January 5, 2023

This is something I wasn't ready for, none of us were ready for. Over the past nine days on this leg of our journey, so many emotions have bubbled up. Fear, pain, tears, love, laughter, joy, ugliness, and beauty all run into one another in a collision of honest emotion.

The grieving is heavy as we wait for answers. The answers never seem to come. We get snippets of information and try not to come to our own conclusions.

We wait. We talk. We develop scenarios. We make mental notes and plans and then go back to what we know. We know nothing except what they think. They pass around hypotheses that sound frightening, in a casual way. Like it's no big deal.

Inside my mind is screaming . . . "How much longer? We just need to know." The waiting is agony but also leaves room for hope. I will hold onto hope. In these moments, I know joy and pain can coexist, maybe even holding each other's hands.

January 9, 2023

If you love something, love it completely, cherish it, say it, but most importantly, show it.
Life is finite & fragile, & just because something is there for one day, it might not be the next.
Never take that for granted.
Say what you need to say, then say a little more. Say too much. Show too much.
Love too much. Everything is temporary but love.
Love outlives us all.
—Author unknown

January 10, 2023

Time
Time is precious.

Time moves the same each and every day. It never moves faster or slower; it just keeps ticking without regard for our plans.

Time can trick us into thinking it moves too slowly when we are excited for something to happen, or time can trick us into thinking it moves too fast when we are anxious about something we don't want to happen. The reality is time moves

Chapter 12

consistently forward, and we only have the time we are given, not more, not less.

For me in these days and weeks, we find ourselves living in something that we didn't plan for or want. This moment is teaching us to use our time wisely, not to rush or wish it away. To live within our time, to love within our time, to give within our time, to be kind within our time, to say the things we need to say within our time and to do our part, to be in each moment within the time we are given.

In the end, I think we all wish we had just a little more time. It's the action that you choose within time that matters.

Time is precious.

January 12, 2023
"We Two"
by Kathie Powell

(To the woman married to the man John shares his room with)

We two strangers in the darkness of a hospital room . . . we two both sit watching, listening, loving, waiting, updating, and praying.

We two are wives of men whom we two have loved for a lifetime.

We two are wives of men in the end stages of cancer.

We two are together yet apart.

We two are on similar paths yet different journeys.

We two catch each other's gaze; we two see each other's pain.

We two exchange no words, yet we two know.
We two have a quiet connection, one we never wanted yet somehow need.
We two are not alone.
We two have each other.
We two are no longer strangers . . . we two.

January 13, 2023

"You Are My Home"
by Kathie Powell

Home . . . my heart's home is with you.
My heart belongs to you.
Each piece of my broken heart is yours.
You are my home.
You will always be my home.
Fear creeps in as the days in this place move along and we are waiting to bring you home. Some days feel like two in one and others like minutes.
Leaving you hurts more than being here watching you slip away . . . I want us to go home.
Then I remember we will always be home together because my heart is yours and your heart is mine.
No matter where we are, our hearts are home.
Home is where the heart is.

Chapter 12

January 14, 2023

Today hasn't been a good day. It was one of the harder more challenging days for John being in his body and one of the harder more challenging days for us as we watched helplessly.

Knowing we are unable to do much for him except be here, call the nurse, hold his hand, ask what he needs, and always tell him we love him. I know he needs that too.

The even harder part is, we have the diagnosis but not any clarity on where he is on this leg of his journey. We speculate and ponder . . . it's so frustrating. We don't have an oncologist to help us understand the process. We have been told it will be six to eight weeks before we will be called for an appointment at the Cross Cancer Clinic. We've also been told by the doctor here that the Cross can't help John; it's too late. (But couldn't they tell us something about what's to come?)

So we continue to walk blind in this storm.

John is so patient and so appreciative of the care he is being given. I am too. We all are. I can't say enough good about the team on this floor who don't specialise in his area of need, giving him such good care.

So as he is being sick and I'm pushing the buzzer to get help, no one is coming. They are so busy. John can see the panic in my eyes, and he says softly, "Don't get impatient. They have so much to do. They'll be here." He squeezes my hand, hangs his head, and continues to retch. I take a deep breath as his wonderful nurse walks in to give him the third round of antinausea meds that he has been given in just a few hours.

He thanks her and says something funny. She laughs and says, "Let's hope this works"

I wait till he says he can lie down again. He is ready to lie down and drifts off to sleep. I pray and pray over him.

Where is the beauty here?

The beauty is in John; it's always in him.

I hate this. I want to wake up and I want to be home snuggled up with him and Wendel, watching a show. But that is not our reality, so I sit in the dark watching my beautiful husband sleep, listening to his breathing. The most beautiful sound I know.

January 17, 2023

Our love language plays a huge role in how we support grieving people. Being support people for our grieving friends, we want to be there for them, and usually, we naturally fall into a supportive place using our love language. All love languages have a place at the grief table. It's also really good to know the grieving person's love language to help guide you in your support of them.

- Words of affirmation: Encouragement
- Acts of service: Anything they need done—taking care of the business of things, shovelling, errands and walking the dog, to name a few
- Gifts—Sending flowers or meals
- Quality time—Sitting with them as they need
- Physical touch—Hugs

Come as you are. Support as needed. Being you, it's just right. You being there as you is just right.

January 18, 2023

This is us now. Cancer has aggressively entered our reality. John is here in the hospital. Tonight, I get to stay here with him; this is our temporary home for now. It's not pretty, the beds aren't comfortable, and it's kinda dull, but the room service is amazing.

None of us are given a guarantee of time, of adventure, of fulfilling our goals and dreams, or of finding our heart's true love. I get that now more than ever.

I get not chasing another moment in the hopes of it being better or like things used to be, so with that understanding, I try to be in the moment. But grief can make me jump ahead or slip behind, taking me out of the moment I'm in. I don't panic about that or get angry with myself. I have an understanding that this is my emotional response when things are overwhelming and in my knowing I can get back to the moment a little faster.

I understand how very blessed I am amidst the most painful journey I've ever been on because I have lived all of the above goals, dreams, adventures, and love with him, and we continue to live our dream even in this place, even in this heartbreak. He is my moment, my past, and my future. He is my now. He is my everything.

January 21, 2023

Coming Home

The first night home, we were on our own. No home care . . . yet. The ride to get here was bumpy, but watching him look at the landscape and take it all in, I could see he felt like this, too, was another little miracle. When we arrived at the house, his face changed—I think I saw what coming home meant to him.

The night on our own was exhausting for each of us, not the romantic story we had envisioned.

The drive home was very hard on his body. It made him ill. We called the twenty-four-hour care line, and an ambulance was dispatched. With the help of the EMS (end-of-life care), we got him feeling better, and we continued our first night.

We made it through . . .

First official day: First thing, he was ill. We worked with him and made him comfortable. Spoke with home care triage and then got a quick appointment with his home care coordinator. At 11:00 he had his assessment. Then at 1:15 p.m., he met with his doctor for his assessment. Meds were changed, and injectables were introduced. The day was long for John. Our heads were spinning. Then we waited for the next things: delivery of meds from the pharmacy and the new home care nurse to put in the ports in his arms and teach us to do the process. Nervously, each one practised on him (something he so patiently allowed . . . John always has the choice to say no because it's his body).

We did it! We have now graduated to being his home care team doing and knowing things we never ever dreamed we'd do or know. With all this, tensions on the team can get high, and we can snip at one another because we all want everything for him to be done the best way possible. And I wanted to do everything, but I couldn't. I needed help, the help they each so freely gave.

We are all scared.

We always have a window to him . . . no matter where we are on this floor.

We sit with him, we talk with him, we share stories, we laugh, we cry, and while he sleeps, we do not. We have time with him. We watch, we listen, and we pray over him. We love him.

January 22, 2023

Papa

In 2008 you became a grandfather for the first time, a role you were born for. You are a papa to five grandsons and two granddaughters. My phone has hundreds and hundreds of pictures of you with your grandkids.

I remember how you talked about each new grandchild before they were born. You would share your hopes and dreams for each child. You were always excited each time.

I think you knew from the moment you heard the news that you were going to be a "papa" for the first time that this was going to be one of the most important roles of your life. You have always been ready for this role. You are a natural.

The first birth, you were there with us, tracking Sarah's contractions (which became your role in almost all the births of grandchildren), and during the ones we couldn't be in the delivery room for, we were close by. For each birthing experience, you naturally kept us in the know by timing contractions and the time between, always calm and steady. Remember how we all cried when each child was born. Cried tears of pure joy. It was a moment we all believed there had to be a higher power. The miracle of birth.

I know your already big heart kept growing bigger, softer, and more open with each new grandchild. From the moment you first held them, your love was and is limitless.

Hot Wheels, monster trucks, Toopy and Binoo, LEGO freestyle, structured LEGO, storybooks, Barbies, sitting patiently getting your face painted and hair done, Play-Doh, soccer, lacrosse, trips, arts and crafts, walks, hugs, kisses, goofy dances, songs, naps, sleepovers, grilled cheese, the middle finger, giggles, jokes, conversations, life lessons, listening, cheering, and time—these are just a few of the things that come to mind when I think of you as a papa.

You love big in action and deeds. You love with your whole heart. You love without expectation. You love completely. You love well. You have been showing each one how to feel love, show love, honour love, and never force love.

Your face lights up when you hear those beautiful words: "I love you, Papa." And you smile and say back, "I love you too."

I love being a grandparent with you. We are a really good team.

John Peter (Papa), you are so loved.

January 23, 2023

I am trying to manage the grief of each day, working on not jumping ahead to tomorrow. He is still here, and he is still the beautiful, smart, funny, wonderful him. Amidst this nightmare, he is always watching me. He can see when I'm struggling and overwhelmed with trying to do my best to serve him well. To give him a good death. He will gently say, "Just finish this part; you are doing so well. Thank you for taking such good care of me." Even with all he is going through, he is encouraging me and telling me I'm doing a good job.

Just know, my love, I will do whatever I can in my power with the village around me to keep you safe and comfortable in the coming days. I will be here, loving you through, just as you are here, loving me through.

Fuck, I love you!

January 24, 2023

Early in the morning, I didn't know this was your last day.

We are all just walking each other home.
—Ram Dass

You are trusting me to walk you all the way home, my love. It's the most intense, dangerous, unexpected, and painful walk I've never been trained for. This walk doesn't come with a road map or option for the scenic tour. It is scary, hard. I want to quit. I cry, I laugh, I silently scream, I pray, and I hope as we love you and keep walking you home.

Each day is different, never knowing what to expect. You know I have no sense of direction, and you are my true north. My geographical artist. When I'm lost, you always help me find my way back. I'm never lost with you.

I will continue this journey with you until you are home, my love.

January 24, 2023

We lost you.

January 25, 2023

Last night at 7:42 p.m. John Peter Powell, the love of my life, died at home. I held his hand.

He was my steadfast. Our family's steadfast. To describe him in just a few words would be just that: devoted, dependable, steady (always there).

I don't have the words right now to put down. I need to sit with this raw, real grief I am experiencing, and then I can write.

My heart has—our hearts have—been shattered, and at the same time there is a peace knowing he is free from this. Death has taken his body, but death cannot take our love.

Babe, I love you.

Chapter 12

January 26, 2023

Wanting my husband to die was the furthest thing from anything I would have ever thought until this leg of the journey. We didn't have much time to wrap our minds around this whole advanced stage 4 cancer and "There is nothing we can do for you." John was diagnosed on January 8 after being in the hospital since December 28. Timeframes were vague; some said less than a year, months maybe, weeks to days. It came in like a raging, hateful beast, the kind of thing that doesn't care about goodbyes, feelings, or love.

I watched my husband slip away more each day, trying to fight to be here for us so we could say all the things we needed to say and he could do the same. We did that over and over. Beautiful messages came in for him, showering him with so much love and appreciation. He got overwhelmed. He has always been so selfless. I told him if there was ever a time to be selfish, this was it. We had said what we felt we needed to, and we had no regrets. Our love will live on; death takes a body, not the love.

He only asked me one thing, and that was to be there with him, holding his hand. I honoured that for him and for me. On Tuesday afternoon, I told him he didn't have to hold on anymore and that we would be okay. That he'd taken care of that. He whispered, "I love you," and I said it back, over and over and over.

He took care of me right up until he couldn't. We were there for each other like always. So yes, in the last few hours of that painful day, I prayed for him to let go and be with Jesus as my heart cried out, "No, how do I do this without you? But how can I ask you to endure one more minute of this?"

In the end, John took the reins and took his last breath. And after the shock and realisation, I was so grateful it was over for him . . . and devastated that my best friend and the love of my life had died.

Grief is full of conflicting feelings . . . waves and gut punches. Memories and laughter, tears and sorrow. Grief is love, and it will go on. This pain I am carrying, I am feeling so I can let it go to move forward, knowing it is and will be different and I am and will be forever changed.

January 28, 2023

"In the Quiet of the Morning"
by Kathie Powell

I wake, it's early, it's still empty
I roll over and snuggle the dog who has taken up half of the bed, your half
In the quiet of the morning

I kiss his furry face, he nuzzles mine
I smile in the dark
The floor is cold as I grab my robe to cover up
With slippers on, I head downstairs in the quiet of the morning

I turn on a light
The room is now in a soft glow
I turn on the fire but it's still cold
I make myself a coffee
I sit with our dog at my feet in the quiet of morning

Your chair is empty
Your slippers there
The feel of you lingers everywhere
My heart keeps breaking silently in the quiet of the morning

The days are long but the nights even longer
I stumble around knowing what today holds
More of the ache, the longing, the pain so deep it brings me to my knees
My anguish is everywhere, even beyond the quiet of the morning

You are gone and I'm alone
We are meant to be together, we are meant to be forever
In the quiet of the morning, in the noise of the day, in the darkness of the night.

January 30, 2023

Anyone can make you smile, many people can make you cry, but it takes someone really special to make you smile with tears in your eyes.
—Unknown

Tired. My bones are tired. I'm overwhelmingly tired these past few days after twenty-eight days of little to no sleep. That's gotta be it. I will sit, and that's it. I'm out. My eyes get so heavy that they hurt. I sleep but somehow don't feel rested. I snuggle up in the blanket I brought for him to have in the hospital so he could have something from home. We brought this blanket home with him. It covered him when he took his last breath. I need this blanket. I want to feel close to him.

I pray to meet with him in my sleep but nothing. No dreams, no message, no him.

I wake, and he is not here either. I wish I could wake up from this nightmare. I wish I could feel his hand in mine, hear his giggle after teasing me (I always set him up well), receive that sweet good morning kiss, or just look over and see him there.

It's the oddest thing. I feel nothing one minute and then so much the next. Joy and pain intertwined in my unsettled, lonely heart and mind.

When I stop trying to create a moment, I do feel him, not in the Hollywood sense . . . in the fact that he is everywhere I turn. His presence is always here with me. Again, I am learning to lean into the moments, not jump ahead, because I miss so much. He taught me that.

I love you, John Peter. Forever.

April 13, 2023

This grief thing . . . am I right?

There are points in this when I feel like I'm going to completely fall apart—oh, and I do. Cool. Then there are points where I only fall apart a little. Like at the pet store when they ask, "How's John? We haven't seen him in a while." That's when I make us all feel uncomfortable. Cool.

There are days when I feel nothing; I'm numb. They say that numbness doesn't last long . . . well, mine comes and goes. I'm not sure why, but it still happens, and on days like that, I can get a lot done. So numb days for me are productive days until something activates my mind into remembering this is all real, and things won't ever be the same. Cue the emotional roller coaster and a one-on-one meeting with my grief. Cool.

There is no one right way to go through this; the only thing we can do is go through it how we go through it.

There will be good days. Don't feel guilty for feeling joy. There will be painful days. Don't feel guilty for feeling sad. There will be days of a bunch of emotions. Don't feel guilty for being emotionally unpredictable.

What I'm trying to say is: don't expect to be over it or handle it better or think, "I've gone through all the stages [there aren't stages]; I shouldn't feel this way." You will feel how you feel, so get acquainted with those feelings, meet with them, see and feel them as you move through the pain to the next feeling. We will feel what we need to feel, even if we try to stuff it down . . . those feelings come out in ways we can't control. Grief will demand your attention and get it without your permission. Grief can be like a child trying to get your attention. You know how they will start off trying to get your attention in a soft, gentle way, then move on to a loud, angry outburst if you are ignoring them? Cool.

Hey, you are walking through your grief one step at a time, in your own way, without a GPS. No road map. Yeah, you are. You are braver than you know. Being brave doesn't mean doing it without fear or emotional pain. Bravery is when you keep going amidst your fear and your emotional pain.

One Year Later: March 31, 2024

"Our Last Expression of Love"
By Kathie Powell
Grief doesn't leave us.
It is a constant companion.
We are forever changed by it.
Grief ebbs and flows, moves and changes.
It is not a structure we are stuck in.
It is something we carry.
Grief is not to be feared or hidden.
Grief needs to be embraced.
Grief is our last expression of love.

Chapter 13
Where Did She Go?

Finding Yourself: The Journey Back to the Real You

"Embrace the suck" is a military quote John used to say in difficult situations. He felt that to *embrace the suck* meant to face and confront the thing that makes you uncomfortable so that you can overcome it. Your job is to learn from it, acknowledge it, and move with it, carrying the lesson it taught you. I don't know about you, but I am not a fan of embracing the suck. But here we go. I would like to preface that grief gets a bad name.

Some people say, "Grief sucks." Grief doesn't suck. Grief hurts. Grief is hard work, but grief is love. Love is beautiful.

Somewhere along the line, I lost my footing. Maybe it was in the days up to the last twenty-eight days or the last twenty-eight days themselves. Or is it since he died? Maybe all the above. I've let go of finding the old me; she is long gone. Sure, parts of her remain. A lot of her remains, but there is something very different about this new me, the woman who lost a part of herself when he died. I'm finding that as I begin to embrace the realness of myself, I'm uncovering the real messy stuff, all the things I've buried and hidden. It all needs to come to the surface. I am learning to grab ahold of my broken heart, hug the woman in the mirror who has aged ten to twenty years with John dying and who has maybe gotten a little rounder as she numbs herself with food.

I didn't lose all of me; I lost the love of my life. I'm still me, different, maybe a little less whole, but maybe whole in a completely different way. Instead of being embraced by him, I am embraced by my grief and forever changed by it.

In life we are always evolving. Events in life change us, and we grow. Losing someone we love is life changing, and we can feel so lost. I don't think we lose ourselves completely. Yes, we have changed, and we will continue to change and grow as we live our lives. Who were you five years ago? Are you a little different? Are you the same person you were before you had kids or before your career or the world shut down that one time? You probably have done or learned something to change the course of your life or your perspective. Living life fully will change us, and loving someone changes us, and losing someone changes us. Maybe you have changed a little from the person you were a few years ago, either by choice or by circumstance.

There have been changes in your life that create room for growth. Now it's time to create room for your grief.

We love, and it hurts sometimes.

Chapter 13

Margery Williams Bianco says it best in this excerpt from pages six and seven of her book *The Velveteen Rabbit:*[1]

"Real isn't how you are made," said the Skin Horse. "It's a thing that happens to you. When a child loves you for a long, long time, not just to play with, but REALLY loves you, then you become Real."

"Does it hurt?" asked the Rabbit.

"Sometimes," said the Skin Horse, for he was always truthful. "When you are Real you don't mind being hurt."

"Does it happen all at once, like being wound up," he asked, "or bit by bit?"

"It doesn't happen all at once," said the Skin Horse. "You become. It takes a long time. That's why it doesn't happen often to people who break easily, or have sharp edges, or who have to be carefully kept. Generally, by the time you are Real, most of your hair has been loved off, and your eyes drop out and you get loose in the joints and very shabby. But these things don't matter at all, because once you are Real you can't be ugly, except to people who don't understand."

"I suppose you are real?" said the Rabbit. And then he wished he had not said it, for he thought the Skin Horse might be sensitive. But the Skin Horse only smiled.

---

1. Margery Williams, The Velveteen Rabbit (London, England: Egmont Books, 2004).

"The Boy's Uncle made me Real," he said. "That was a great many years ago; but once you are Real you can't become unreal again. It lasts for always."

After everything you have been through, you are real.

Grief is a reflection of the love you shared. Big love brings big grief, but it isn't the end. I don't think you lose all of yourself when someone you love dies, but there is a huge part missing, and that's where the change is. You don't fill that missing part; you learn to embrace it. Here are some things I incorporated to help me with the process of coming back to what's left of me, to embracing who I am now.

Some of these ideas might resonate with you or not. The key is to find your own way and try some things, some might work and some might not. It's okay to try.

- Guided imagery.(youtube has some amazing ones to try)
- Get dressed and get into nature for a walk. Being alone in these moments makes this space a good time to think and reflect.
- Write, write, write, and get those thoughts on paper. (Visit www.kathiepowell.ca for a free ten page journal.)
- Pat yourself on the back for the little wins in your day. Celebrate your path towards healing. Baby steps are still steps in the direction you are going.
- Think about what is meaningful to you now. Is it the same as before, or has it changed? Embrace it and start

taking steps to create something more out of what is meaningful to you. Creating a legacy project: What do you want people to hold onto when they remember you? What is your legacy?
- Take that trip. Book it and go.
- Do something you never had time for before. Learn something new.
- Give yourself permission to live and embrace life a little at a time.
- Give yourself permission to cry.
- Be honest; it's the only way you will truly find the truth in who you are.

When it's time, give yourself permission to rediscover yourself by doing some soul searching. Finding yourself won't be without challenges, but it has so many possibilities.

The woman I am today has embraced the challenge of self-discovery. Digging into what's hidden and uncomfortable. The me without him. I have confronted and embraced my grief. I've become comfortable in the uncomfortable. I am a brave, independent risk-taker. I am unafraid to try new things. I keep the people I love close. I am not about making everyone happy. I've learned it's not my responsibility. I have set boundaries and kept them. I love to spend hours with my grandchildren. I am adventurous. I might just join a rock band again. Who knows?

I am having fun. I am creative and carefree, and I have a renewed purpose. I also am sad, and I weep when something pierces my heartstrings. I am real. I am worn but not worn out.

The Hardest, Not the Worst Year

I am building on his legacy of love, service, and giving back. I know my heart will always love John, forever. With that knowledge, I am boldly living my life with a broken heart. I trust her. I've never said that before and meant it. I had to learn to trust her; she is all I have.

Grief is a close and trusted friend. Grief comes with me wherever I go.

I love a purposeful, hard conversation. I say what I need to say to the people I love. I am unapologetically vulnerable. I don't have to fit to belong. I am perfectly imperfect with my grief interwoven into my heart. I am still me. I've been knocked down; the bottom fell out, and I got back up—a little worse for wear—but I am here, embracing this life as it is now. Heart open, feet planted, and eyes open wide enough to see the real beauty of my life woven together with my grief. They are not separate.

In the aftershock of losing John, the journey to rediscovering myself has been anything but easy. It's taken resilience, an openness to living with a broken heart, and the courage to believe I stand tall on my own. This past year has been the hardest, not the worst year of my life, but through it all, I've come to embrace the beauty of life in a way I never thought possible.

I have a grief moment to share here. I grieve that he is missing this person I'm becoming. I know he would have really been proud of her.

I encourage you to be honest as you dig into the hard stuff. You need to be brave here; this is hard work. Just know you are there within yourself, embraced by love and grief.

Chapter 13

Embracing this me has required hard work and dedication. It's meant facing my fears head-on and allowing myself to feel every emotion, even the ones that hurt the most. It's meant taking risks and stepping outside of my comfort zone, even when every fibre of my being wanted to retreat into the safety of the familiar, but nothing is the same.

Through it all, I've learned that being brave doesn't mean never feeling afraid; it means facing those fears with courage and determination. It means allowing myself to be vulnerable, even when it's the last thing I want to do. And it means embracing the journey, even when the road ahead seems daunting and uncertain. It means trusting myself.

Today, as I look back on the past year, I am filled with gratitude for the lessons I've learned and the person I've become. I may have lost a part of myself when I lost John, but in the process, I've found a strength and resilience I never knew I had. Something he saw in me. As I continue to embrace my life, I do so with a renewed sense of purpose and a deep appreciation for the beauty of each moment, keeping the memory of him alive in me.

Somewhere along the line, I decided to start writing. I joined a book group, and like most things, it was too soon. I wasn't ready to pour out what was stuck inside. But it was a purposeful process; it brought me here to meet with me. She was there within the words. I also decided to invest in what I do. I am a grief coach. I know and understand grief. I loved walking with grievers, but I did need to step back from coaching because I couldn't give back just yet. I needed to work on my own healing journey.

The gift of healing shows differently for all of us. I processed a lot by sharing our story on Instagram. The most amazing thing was this community started growing with me, and I could process with them listening, but no one was interrupting me. Other grievers started reaching out, finding their voice in mine. The truth is, we grievers need to be heard and not be fixed. It has been helpful for me because I was being heard, and others were feeling seen. They had finally found a place they could open up. It was and is the most beautiful feeling to open a door to let our grief out and let others' grief in.

So I began my long, complicated, and challenging journey to the top of the mountain to meet the person I was becoming. She is in the longing, the longing for him and the longing to learn more. I started my search to find out more about dying and death. Why was everything so secret? Why didn't people talk about something that we will all experience at some point? True story: We all have an expiration date. So why not talk about it?

I began my first end-of-life (EOL) doula course, which opened a deeper wound of losing John. There was so much I didn't know, and now I was learning the realities of dying and death. There is beauty to be held here. So much we can do together to prepare and create a space full of love and honour. It doesn't take the pain of losing someone away; it just creates a space that is free from fear because understanding something takes the fear away.

Chapter 13

I have since taken two other end-of-life doula programs with two authors and EOL doulas that I admire so much. Each has brought more richness to my offering and to my life.

I decided I wanted to get some help being more intentional with my business, so I got a coach, and she was such a gift. Through her, I've found even more of my purpose. I also got a woman to set up my new website, which I am so proud of. So in a year where I was plagued by fear, I stepped out in that fear and created a room for grievers, dying people, and their families to learn, grow, feel seen, feel safe, and to begin to live fully till they die. The woman I'm becoming is right here, and I really like her. I think John would like her too.

None of this would have happened without John's death. I didn't choose the path; it chose me. I am here to honour this newfound purpose and live my life fully and completely as I peel back the layers to finding me.

I won't lie; finding me is not just about a new purpose or learning to operate a whipper snipper. There are so many things to unpack. Looking at my future, I wonder: Will I be alone forever? Is that a good thing or not so good? So in the process of self-discovery, I thought maybe I should look at finding a companion. Maybe dating? Yeah, twelve months in, I'm thinking, "I'm good; I think I might want to find a companion." The thought of this whole thing terrifies me but also gives me hope. Time is time, and there is no timeline on this part of the journey either. Some of us will embrace new relationships, and others may not. Neither is wrong. *Wait, what?*

Stepping into the world of dating after losing the love of your life can feel like navigating shark-infested waters. My impression of dating sites is that they are awful. I find it's like looking for a rescue animal (I don't need rescuing), only the pictures aren't as good. It's online shopping. It's a journey marked by vulnerability, uncertainty, and a multitude of emotions. The honest truth is, it's scary. For me, it's more than just trying to find a connection. How the heck do I do this at my age? I am sixty-two. I have a sixty-two-year-old body, mind, and spirit (okay, most times I act like I'm a teenager, but my hips don't lie). The honest truth is I grew old with John; we grew older together. We were together when our bodies weren't ravaged by life. We aged together beautifully, I think. I knew and loved his body through the ages and he mine. I don't know how to start dating at this age with this body. Yes, I have concerns, but honestly, my body is the least important thing about me. Trust is a huge thing, and it takes time to build. I know I'm not ready for any kind of intimacy. It's okay not to be ready. Healing takes work; it is a personal journey that unfolds at its own pace. There's no right or wrong timeline for when or if you dip your toes into the dating pool. It's okay to try. Exploring new connections doesn't diminish the love you shared with your forever. Something I've learned is that we have the capacity to open our hearts to love again, in whatever form it may take. It doesn't have to be romantic love.

Dating after loss may or may not be for me. It's about honouring my own needs, boundaries, and readiness to

Chapter 13

embrace new possibilities. I get that there is no one-size-fits-all approach to love and relationships. There is no one-size-fits-all approach to life. It's completely unique. So to anyone navigating the complexities of dating after loss, know that you're not alone. Take each step at your own pace, be gentle with yourself, and remember that it's okay to feel whatever you're feeling along the way. You're worthy of love, and your journey deserves to be honoured and respected.

For now, the love of family and current friends is filling my cup as I hold onto the love I carry for John. My heart is full of him. I'm not disappointed that I tried. I know now I'm not ready, and I may never be. Being alone with the person I'm becoming is more than okay. Like I said before, I like her, and she is enough.

Grief has a way of consuming us, clouding our vision, and making it difficult to see beyond the pain. But through the tears and the heartache, we can find strength we never knew we had. We are resilient. We are on a journey of self-discovery, of learning to navigate life's twists and turns without the person we once thought we couldn't live without. Here we are, living without them, something I bet you never thought was possible until you found yourself here.

The gift of self-discovery is knowing that embracing your grief brings you to a place where you find yourself without all the layers of "I'm fine" piled on. Underneath is where you will find you. The real you. Know you can live your life fully even with a broken heart. Showing your grief is not a sign of weakness; it's a sign of love.

One Last Journal Entry: January 24, 2024

It's Been a Year

When you lose the love of your life, things shift, and the change is big. You learn so much about yourself, so much you didn't know. You learn how life isn't just about going through the motions, merely existing day to day. It's about embracing every opportunity, big or small, to truly live—to savour the taste of each moment, to inhale deeply the scent of possibility, and to dive headfirst into the depths of experience. It's about chasing dreams with unwavering passion, connecting with others in meaningful ways, and finding beauty in the most unexpected places. It's about the missteps and mistakes, the wins and losses. It's all the moments that make a day a day.

John did not settle for merely existing; he was about living with intention, purpose, and love. So while I'm still living, I am going to make every heartbeat count, every breath a celebration of the boundless richness of life in all its beautiful messiness. I am going to live till I die.

In the quiet of our lives, grief whispers its presence, yet our conversations about grief remain hushed, as if we are afraid to confront its raw reality. But grief is not something to be hidden in the shadows; it needs to come into the light to reveal to us the depth of our love, the ache of our loss, and the power within us to embrace this life without them.

I will not whisper or hush my grief. I did not whisper or hush my love.

"Living till I die"

Chapter 14
Losing a Father

A Daughter's Grief

Losing someone you love affects the whole family, those connected by blood and those chosen as family. Each person experiences loss differently because our grief is tied to the unique relationship we shared with the person who passed away. Even though we all lost John, each of us lost someone different—a father, a grandfather, a son-in-law, a friend, and even our beloved dog Wendel. Over the next few pages, you will read my daughters' different experiences with their grief; it is very clear how unique their grief is to their relationship with their father. Some questions weren't answered by each because it was too painful. I honour that.

Our Daughters' Points of View

How would you describe your relationship with your dad?

SARAH. Dad and I were super close. I'd go to him for anything—questions, advice, you name it. He was my rock, and I always wanted to make him proud. He never let me doubt his love for me.

RAYNA. I know without a shadow of a doubt that he loved me and he was proud of me, and I felt the same way. We loved to banter and bug each other, but also could have really deep conversations. I always felt safe and loved when I was around him.

What has been the hardest part of losing your dad?

SARAH. It's like he's always on my mind. If I'm not thinking about him, I feel guilty, like I'm forgetting him. It's tough to focus on anything for too long because I keep going back to those last months with him.

RAYNA. I don't know; it's all so hard. I could write a whole list of reasons. Maybe it would be the fact that it felt way too soon. Like he should still be here. And it happened so fast.

JILL. Not having him around for advice or his jokes.

What do you remember about the night your father died?

SARAH. I remember feeling despair like I've never felt before. Disbelief and despair. I can feel it creep up in the back of my throat right now. Like I knew, we all knew, it was coming, but when it actually did, I didn't want to believe it. I don't know if I can describe it any better than that.

Chapter 14

RAYNA. Feeling incredibly anxious and knowing something was different—really knowing, deep down, that he was dying. Being really stressed that it seemed none of the health care workers were taking me seriously and trying my best to help in whatever way I could to keep Dad comfortable. I remember seeing him struggling, my mom crying out for me to call the nurse and get someone here, trying to warm up his sheet in the dryer ... feeling like I needed to try to at least help him keep warm. My heart was breaking. Jay came home with the medication ... me telling my dad with a pit in my stomach that I was giving him medicine and praying to God that it would help. Standing over him and feeling his last breath in my hand, feeling him leave. "Smoke on the Water" playing. Jay helped take his ring off. Mom cut a lock of his hair.

JILL. I remember I had just put Zach to bed, then I was putting Gus to bed, and I heard Jarret talking, and I thought Zach had woken up, even though I didn't hear him crying. I came downstairs and heard your voice talking to Jarret, and I knew in the pit of my stomach that Dad had died because you were calling so late. I remember asking Rayna to let me see Dad, and thinking he looked like he was just sleeping. I remember sleeping downstairs with Zach and crying on and off all night.

What do you remember about the celebration of life?
SARAH. It all felt like a dream. I felt disconnected, like I was watching it all from afar. It was awful.
RAYNA. Not much. It was honestly such a blur, and I was numb. In disbelief.
JILL. It's all a blur to me.

How hard was it going back to your old life?
SARAH. Really hard. Everything feels off, especially outside of home and family. It's tough to see life moving on without him.
RAYNA. So hard. I remember just thinking how do I do this? How does life just carry on? It was, and honestly still at times, is incredibly hard to reconcile and navigate.
JILL. I don't think I ever will.

Have you made any big changes since he died?
SARAH. I quit my job and went back to school for a new career. I just couldn't keep doing what I was doing before.
RAYNA. I have in terms of who I spend time with or worry about . . . family is everything to me, and I feel like we've all gotten so much closer. I don't try to force relationships at all anymore or try to overextend myself. Life is too short.
JILL. No.

Chapter 14

What have you kept that was his and why?

SARAH. I have some of his clothes and lots of photos. I even got one of his writings tattooed on my arm: "I love you."

RAYNA. A lot of clothing actually! An airborne shirt, a Be Bold sweatshirt, a James Taylor hoodie, sweatpants, slippers, things like that.

JILL. Some of his shirts.

Have you felt him or had signs he is near?

SARAH. No, I haven't.

RAYNA. I have. We all recently got 11:11 tattoos because of how often we see it pop up. For me, the most significant time was when Jay was wheeling me out of the hospital after emergency surgery in June, and above the door, the clock read 11:11. I also really feel his presence when I go on walks outdoors by myself.

JILL. I dream about him sometimes.

Over time, has your grief gotten easier?

SARAH. Not really. It comes and goes, but the sadness is always there.

RAYNA. I don't think it does, I think what happens is your tolerance becomes greater. Maybe that's not the right way to describe it, but you're just more used to carrying it. It can still hit you like a ton of bricks anytime, though.

JILL. No, it hasn't.

What are your go-to coping skills?
SARAH. I withdraw from everyone and everything. I don't want to hurt the people I love.
RAYNA. For me, fitness. Working out, movement, yoga, walking, lifting weights.
JILL. Drawing.

Has your relationship changed with your husband?
SARAH. We got even closer during Dad's illness and after he passed away. It was a special bond we shared.
RAYNA. Yes. I am a lot more aware of what matters. I definitely appreciate him more and try to be more present.

What have you noticed about your children's grief?
SARAH. They're all coping differently, but it's been tough for each of them.
RAYNA. That it is unfiltered, and we can all learn so much from that. That they want to talk about him and remember him, and we need to show them that it is okay to do that.
JILL. My youngest doesn't seem to fully grasp it yet.

Do you feel comfortable talking about your grief?
SARAH. Not really. It's hard to put into words.
RAYNA. For me, it honestly depends on who I am with. I feel like it is a pretty sacred thing, and not everyone can hold space or, frankly, deserves to have access to that part of you . . . especially if they can't honour it.

Chapter 14

JILL. Not really.

What do you worry about now?
SARAH. Making decisions without Dad's guidance.
RAYNA. Worry is hard. I feel my anxiety has gotten so much worse since Dad died. Anticipatory grief, worry, and just having a greater understanding of the fragility of life and the finality of death. It really changes you. You worry about your people a lot more.
JILL. How my own death will affect my kids.

What has grief taught you?
SARAH. To cherish the people you love while you can. It's made me reflect on what truly matters in life.
RAYNA. Such a tough question. I feel like right now, it's taught me that the pain of loss is so immense, and it's also very transformative. That you enter into a world, or experience that people who have not yet experienced significant loss cannot understand. So you gain a new perspective. You see everything differently. You can't go back, and it can really separate you from others who might not get it because you can't pretend you don't know.

My daughters were there for their father in a way only they could be there. One was the caregiver; one was the administrator, doing what he needed done there; and one was the support. They each gave him so much love, and in return, he gave each of them his.

Wendel (Our Dog)

Wendel can't write, so I will do it for him, actions speak louder than words. He had a deep bond and connection to John.

Even before John's passing, Wendel sensed something was wrong. He would bark at him and get very animated, like we needed to go and do something. He did this frequently. It is said that animals can sense illness. I believe they can.

During John's last moments, Wendel stayed close, keeping vigil outside the room. When John was actively dying, Wendel tried to get on to the bed. I wish I had let him.

Since then, Wendel has shown signs of grief too. He's been more anxious, barking more and generally being a very alert guard dog. I took him to the vet, and she asked me if I talked to Wendel about what happened and where John is. I hadn't. She told me he is confused about where John went and when he is coming back. So that day when we got home, I took Wendel to John's urn and we talked. I can't say for sure, but after that day, maybe I felt better telling him because he's slowly finding his footing again. He is still my guard dog, and I appreciate that so much.

Wendel lost his best friend too. Animals grieve, and they feed off our energy. It's important to acknowledge any behaviours or things that are out of the ordinary and give them

Chapter 14

some extra love and attention—just like they do with us. A dog will comfort you when you need it most.

This chapter is to remind us that everyone's grief is unique and valid. We process differently, and our relationship is special to us. No one else will feel quite like we do. Sometimes we can recognise similar expressions of feelings. We don't compare because we are not the same. The experience of sharing our grief connects us. By sharing our stories and supporting each other, we honour the love and loss we've experienced. Grief is a heart thing. When we are there for each other, listening without judgement or comparison, we open the door to healing.

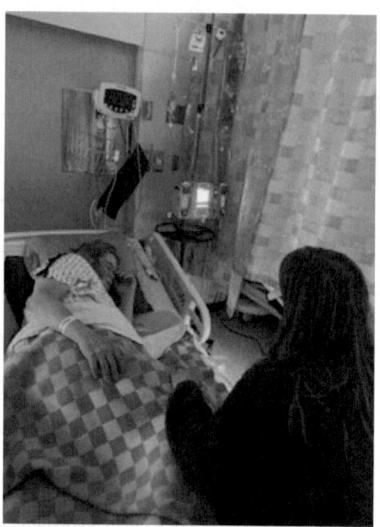

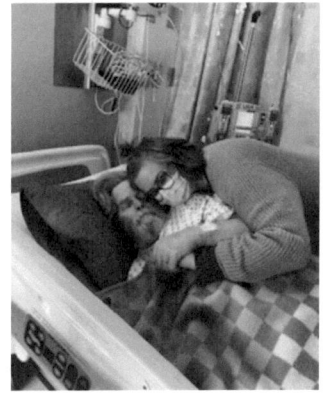

"Family"

Epilogue
The Last First Time

Dear John

In the weeks and days leading up to this moment in time, things really shifted for me. I felt like I was back in the throes of last year. I was back in the pain of it. I couldn't figure out what was happening. Yes, what was wrong with me? Oh right, grief . . . so nothing is wrong with me. I don't know about you, but I am finding as the weeks approach a certain marker (anniversary)—whatever you want to call them—I get very uneasy. In December, we went through Christmas, and before Christmas, I didn't even want a tree. I didn't want to celebrate. I didn't want to be with anyone. What was there to celebrate? Jonn made Christmas for me and our family. It was about the moments and surprises. He always got me something very special. I loved his surprises.

After spending time with my girls and grandkids, I realised I wanted to be with my family, even if I was a mess. We all wanted to be together. So I got myself three little trees,

The Hardest, Not the Worst Year

simple but pretty. I didn't over decorate, and to be honest, on Christmas morning before everyone got there, I had the trees down. I needed to get my space back. We all gathered at my house and had a wonderful meal. Jay prepared the turkey; he took over John's role. He made the dressing exactly like John, and the turkey was perfect. The dressing was something my father passed on to John, and now Jay has taken it over. I cried when I tasted it because Jay had captured the taste and the texture. It was a moment when we could feel John's presence. He would have been so proud. Our Christmas was beautiful and sad. I'm so glad we spent it together.

Our next big marker was the one-year mark. The whole month felt raw, and it was hard to go through. I wanted to run away from all the reminders of the past year. I can honestly say in the month of January, I remembered everything about where I was, what I was doing and how I was feeling the year before. It all flooded back to me.

During this time, my sister lost her husband to cancer. December was a difficult month for many reasons, and this was part of the story. Their story. Walking with my sister and her husband a year after she had walked with me on a similar journey with John. How was something like this even possible or fair? I can't answer that. Mike died with Maggie looking into his eyes, telling him she loved him and it was okay to go. I swear to God, I felt like I had left my body and was seeing myself for the first time a year ago when John took his last breath. I shook my head and came back to her. It wasn't about me. I prayed silently over her as he took his last breath. Devastated, we stayed for a moment, but then she said, "He is gone; this is not him. I want to go." So we walked out of the hospital at about 5:30 a.m on January 3, 2024.

We walked to the car, and we drove away in disbelief but still knowing what we had just been a part of. Because we had driven into the hospital the night before, it would be simple to navigate home: just go straight. It was dark, and I started driving. We turned off the GPS because we knew where we were going. I drove us home—or so I thought. The trip in the dark seemed to take longer than when we drove in. Yes, we got lost. There was one turn at the beginning we missed. Why would I turn off the GPS at a time like this when, on a normal day, neither of us had a sense of direction? We were nowhere near my sister's house. I realised that when a sign pointed to a town I didn't know. So I put the GPS on and headed home the long way. We laughed because we imagined John and Mike looking down on us and thinking, "Really?"

Once we got back to her house. We sat for a bit. Then she paced. I had a shower, and we just sat for a while, and then she sent me home. Her son was coming in that night and would be staying with her for the next week. She needed some time alone to process it all, wander, and cry. I got that, and I hugged her as I left. On the way home, I cried for both of us.

January is a month I can't say I want to forget because it holds the last moments I had with him. January wasn't all pain, but it did bring in its fair share.

The Hardest, Not the Worst Year

I talked to the girls about what we should do for the anniversary, if anything. They suggested getting together and maybe lighting sparklers, playing music, and letting some balloons go in his honour. I decided to make one of his favourite meals: lasagna and Caesar salad with garlic bread.

Before we ate, I read a letter to John. As I started to read, Jay said, "Listen." The song on the speaker was *Against the Wind* . . . coincidence? I don't think so. John never liked to miss a family get-together. John's presence was in the room. Everyone was silent as I read the letter and thanked each one for being there for me and each other this year. Some of us cried; others looked off into the distance, but each one of us remembered. John would have been so proud. After I read the letter at around 7:42 p.m., exactly one year from the moment we lost him, we all went outside with the music playing. We lit the sparklers and let the balloons go into the sky, each holding a thought for him in our hearts as we let them float off into the atmosphere. It was beautiful. I will cherish that evening for as long as I live.

The Letter

Dear John,

It's been one year since you left us, since you moved on to heaven. A lot has happened over the past year, which I believe you have probably watched from above. Sometimes, I think I feel your presence. I get little signs when I pay attention. They show up: 11:11 was the first recurring message that showed up

Epilogue

just when I needed it. Then songs randomly showed up, things we loved to listen to together. I would hear, listen, and feel. I know it could be explained away by saying I hit something on my phone when it was in my pocket. But why would the specific song come on if it wasn't some sort of message from you? I choose to believe in the signs. Oh, and the crow. I love that crow. I hope he comes back this spring. I miss him too.

I long to see you in my sleep and meet you in my dreams. I only had one dream of you early on. Maybe I won't get any more dreams of you. But I keep you in my mind's eye and in my heart. I see you in the sunrise and feel you in the sunset.

Lately, I have been longing to touch your face. Just feel your skin. Feel your hand on my hand and your cheek against mine and your lips kissing me softly. To feel the closeness of you. It's not that I haven't had a longing for you over the past year, but lately, it's so much more intense.

My broken heart continues to beat. I continue to live this life. Although everything has changed. And in a strange, maybe beautiful, way, I look at the world just a little more clearly. Not so much with rose-coloured glasses. Some might think I would see more darkness than light. But there is light. There's more light than darkness.

I know you know my heart, but I want to express to you how much I love you. How much I miss you. And how much you are a part of my every thought. Even if it's not in the forefront, your presence is hovering. Your encouragement, your wisdom. Somehow you always show up. You gave me wings when we were together. I felt when you died, my wings had been clipped, but they haven't been. They are still there. They're a little road-weary. A little broken. But I can still fly. You created a life for us that was beyond anything I ever imagined or thought I deserved. With you, my life was so safe, beautiful, and full of the richest purest love.

I miss the safety of you. I miss knowing that I'm going to be okay because I'm with you. But I've learned to rely on myself a little more. To trust myself a little more. And to believe in myself a little more. Something that you always encouraged me to do. To believe that I was worth believing in and trusting. That I could rely on myself. You told me I was going to be okay. And I can tell you, Babe, I'm okay most of the time.

And I guess that's enough. I believe that you are up above and you are looking down on us. Watching over us. Loving us, missing us. My prayer is that it's true and you have a window to watch over all of us, me, your children, and your grandchildren. Watch as they grow and learn and become the people that they were always meant to be. The people you saw. Each one of us carries a part of you within ourselves. I see it every time I'm with any one of them. Your legacy of love and service is ingrained in each one of us. Giving back without having to be noticed for it.

John Peter, I know I've made mistakes over the past year. I've made decisions that you probably wouldn't agree with. As you lay dying, you told me that I could do what I needed to do because you weren't going to be there and it wouldn't matter.

But you know, you are here in my heart, and it does matter to me what you would think about all this. I know, deep down, you would smile. I feel like you would really appreciate everything I've done to work through all this pain. I know you would never make me feel bad for making a decision or choice without you.

So, my love, I know one day I will be with you. I understand the process of death so much better now. I wish I would have understood it more when we were in the midst of it together, but I can't change the past. I can only work towards the future and continue to learn more about grief, dying, and death. I know you would be proud of me for what I am doing. For what I'm trying to do in this world. I love you so much, and I'm going to continue to give back and love on people. Share what I've learned to give people what we didn't have.

In this learning process of transitioning from life to death and all the things that go with it, I hope you know you were the catalyst for the growth I have experienced. I know with everything in my heart and soul that we, your family, did everything we could to honour and love you through your transition, and I think you felt it. I don't know what it's like to be a dying person. I just know what it's like to be the loved one of a dying person. It is the greatest pain that I have ever experienced, and I can only imagine how you felt, being the dying person. It must have been the greatest pain that you'd ever experienced, but also one that you are ready for. You told me you knew where you were going. You weren't afraid. But

. . . we weren't ready. Is anyone ever really ready to lose their everything?

So, my love, I don't know what this next year holds. Maybe more stepping into my purpose and helping others. Writing our story. Honouring you in all that I do and with all that I am, even the anxious, flighty, and emotional parts of me. In life, you never judged me for my emotional parts. You loved me with them, in them, and in spite of them.

I love you, John Peter. I always have, and I always will. And I will miss you until my last breath and you take my hand, leading me home with you. I will always be forever yours.

Love your forever,

Kathleen xxoo x forever

"*my favourite picture of John*"   "*Oreo our new cat*"

"*Sending love*"

Let's Connect

If you are curious about how to work with me or want to connect with me, here's how:

1. By Accessing Your Gift
Workbook Companion to *The Hardest, Not the Worst, Year*. Use your workbook as prompts for your personal journal or for groups like book clubs or grief support groups.

2. By Hiring Me to Speak or Appear on Your Podcast
Email hello@kathiepowell.ca with "SPEAKING" in the subject line.

3. By Connecting on Social Media
The journey doesn't end here. I'd love to connect with you on Instagram, where I post daily reels about grief and my experiences that hopefully resonate and inspire you to share your own story.
You can find me on Instagram at @aroomforgrief.

4. By Reading My Blog

To read my blog, visit my website at www.kathiepowell.ca.

5. By Leaving a Review and Sharing with Loved Ones

If this book touched your heart and made an impact, I would love for you to leave a review wherever you purchased this book, and/or share with anyone you know who is grieving or curious about grief.

6. Listen to My Podcast with Co-Host Kimberley Hiebert

Our podcast, *The Kim And Kath Show*, is a joyful podcast that challenges the norms for aging women, with a mission to start a revolution! Every week we bring laughter (lots of it), experiences, and examples to encourage each of you, as well as ourselves, to live our best lives EVER, no matter what age or stage we are in! Find it on YouTube at https://www.youtube.com/@thekimandkathshow and Instagram @thekimandkathshow, and all popular podcast platforms.

About the Author

Kathie Powell is a mother, a grandmother, a griever, an author, a grief educator/coach/mentor, an end-of-life doula, and a forever learner. And sometimes a jingle writer. She's a terrible knitter, with a love-hate relationship with knitting. If she doesn't say it, her face will. A sing-talker, Kathie doesn't necessarily believe that *all* things happen for a reason, but that no matter what, you can find meaning if you search for it.

She wrote this book because she couldn't find a book for midlife grievers when she needed it most. It's for grievers, for people who know someone who is grieving, and for anyone curious about grief. It was written to help make grief less scary. Grief is part of life. It's a natural human experience.

Kathie helps grieving people using the seven-week online program called The Grief Recovery Method, it is not therapy but is therapeutic in nature. She is a Grief Coach, coaching grievers as they work through the process of life after loss. She listens to their stories without any kind of judgement to help them work through the pain that's holding them back, giving them tools to support them as they continue to walk through life as a griever.

In her work as an end-of-life doula, she creates a safe space for open and honest conversation about dying, death, and grief. She supports both the dying person and their family. Kathie listens to people, serving as a resource to help them advocate for things they need and as someone who can help build legacy projects and plan end-of-life documentation. She believes that grief is not something to hide, and the end of life is not something to be afraid of. Kathie's mission is to empower people to move through loss with the understanding that the depths of grief, while painful, are also a reflection of a great love shared.

Made in the USA
Thornton, CO
07/19/24 03:52:09

50dad9f7-dc3c-4e26-b4fa-b0f9e3bbc07cR01